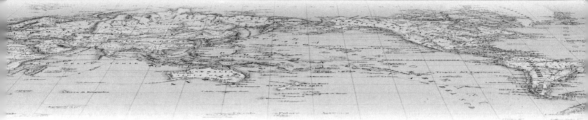

Hernando de Soto

and His Expeditions Across the Americas

Explorers of New Lands

Explorers of New Lands

Hernando de Soto
and His Expeditions Across the Americas

Janet Hubbard-Brown

Series Consulting Editor William H. Goetzmann
Jack S. Blanton, Sr. Chair in History and American Studies
University of Texas, Austin

CHELSEA HOUSE
PUBLISHERS
A Haights Cross Communications Company ®
Philadelphia

COVER: A portrait of Hernando de Soto

CHELSEA HOUSE PUBLISHERS
VP, NEW PRODUCT DEVELOPMENT Sally Cheney
DIRECTOR OF PRODUCTION Kim Shinners
CREATIVE MANAGER Takeshi Takahashi
MANUFACTURING MANAGER Diann Grasse

Staff for HERNANDO DE SOTO
EXECUTIVE EDITOR Lee Marcott
EDITORIAL ASSISTANT Carla Greenberg
PRODUCTION EDITOR Bonnie Cohen
PHOTO EDITOR Sarah Bloom
COVER AND INTERIOR DESIGNER Keith Trego
LAYOUT 21st Century Publishing and Communications, Inc.

A Haights Cross Communications ✦ Company ®

www.chelseahouse.com

First Printing

9 8 7 6 5 4 3 2 1

Library of Congress Cataloging-in-Publication Data

Hubbard-Brown, Janet.
  Hernando de Soto: and his expeditions across the Americas/Janet Hubbard.
    p. cm.—(Explorers of new lands)
  Includes bibliographical references and index.
  ISBN 0-7910-8610-0 (hard cover)
 1. Soto, Hernando de, ca. 1500-1542—Juvenile literature. 2. Explorers—America—
Biography—Juvenile literature. 3. Explorers—Spain—Biography—Juvenile literature.
4. America—Discovery and exploration—Spanish—Juvenile literature. I. Title. II. Series.
  E125.S7H83 2005
  970.01'6'092—dc22
                                                        2005010069

Table of Contents

Introduction

by William H. Goetzmann
Jack S. Blanton, Sr. Chair in History and American Studies
University of Texas, Austin

Explorers have always been adventurers. They were, and still are, people of vision and most of all, people of curiosity. The English poet Rudyard Kipling once described the psychology behind the explorer's curiosity:

"Something hidden. Go and find it. Go and
     look behind the Ranges—
Something lost behind the Ranges. Lost and
     waiting for you. Go!" [1]

Miguel de Cervantes, the heroic author of *Don Quixote*, longed to be an explorer-conquistador. So he wrote a personal letter to King Phillip II of Spain asking to be appointed to lead an expedition to the New World. Phillip II turned down his request. Later, while in prison, Cervantes gained revenge. He wrote the immortal story of *Don Quixote*, a broken-down, half-crazy "Knight of La Mancha" who "explored" Spain with his faithful sidekick, Sancho Panza. His was perhaps the first of a long line of revenge novels—a lampoon of the real explorer-conquistadors.

Most of these explorer-conquistadors, such as Columbus and Cortés, are often regarded as heroes who discovered new worlds and empires. They were courageous, brave and clever, but most of them were also cruel to the native peoples they met. For example, Cortés, with a small band of 500 Spanish conquistadors, wiped out the vast

Aztec Empire. He insulted the Aztecs' gods and tore down their temples. A bit later, far down in South America, Francisco Pizarro and Hernando de Soto did the same to the Inca Empire, which was hidden behind a vast upland desert among Peru's towering mountains. Both tasks seem to be impossible, but these conquistadors not only overcame nature and savage armies, they stole their gold and became rich nobles. More astounding, they converted whole countries and even a continent to Spanish Catholicism. Cathedrals replaced blood-soaked temples, and the people of South and Central America, north to the Mexican border, soon spoke only two languages—Portuguese in Brazil and Spanish in the rest of the countries, even extending through the Southwest United States.

Most of the cathedral building and language changing has been attributed to the vast numbers of Spanish and Portuguese missionaries, but trade with and even enslavement of the natives must have played a great part. Also playing an important part were great missions that were half churches and half farming and ranching communities. They offered protection from enemies and a life of stability for the natives. Clearly vast numbers of natives took to these missions. The missions vied with the cruel native caciques, or rulers, for protection and for a constant food supply. We have to ask ourselves: Did the Spanish conquests raise the natives' standard of living? And did a religion of love appeal more to the natives than ones of sheer terror, where hearts were torn out and bodies were tossed down steep temple stairways as sacrifices that were probably eaten by dogs or other wild beasts? These questions are something to think about as you read the Explorers of New Lands series. They are profound questions even today.

"New Lands" does not only refer to the Western Hemisphere and the Spanish/Portuguese conquests there. Our series should probably begin with the fierce Vikings—Eric the Red, who discovered Greenland in 982, and Leif Ericson, who discovered North America in 1002, followed, probably a year later, by a settler named Bjorni. The Viking sagas (or tales passed down through generations) tell the stories of these men and of Fredis, the first woman discoverer of a New Land. She became a savior of the Viking men when, wielding a broadsword and screaming like a madwoman, she single-handedly routed the native Beothuks who were about to wipe out the earliest Viking settlement in North America that can be identified. The Vikings did not, however, last as long in North America as they did in Greenland and Northern England. The natives of the north were far tougher than the natives of the south and the Caribbean.

Far away, on virtually the other side of the world, traders were making their way east toward China. Persians and Arabs as well as Mongols established a trade route to the Far East via such fabled cities as Samarkand, Bukhara, and Kashgar and across the Hindu Kush and Pamir Mountains to Tibet and beyond. One of our volumes tells the story of Marco Polo, who crossed from Byzantium (later Constantinople) overland along the Silk Road to China and the court of Kublai Khan, the Mongol emperor. This was a crossing over wild deserts and towering mountains, as long as Columbus's Atlantic crossing to the Caribbean. His journey came under less dangerous (no pirates yet) and more comfortable conditions than that of the Polos, Nicolo and Maffeo, who from 1260 to 1269 made their way across these endless wastes while making friends, not enemies, of the fierce Mongols. In 1271, they took along Marco Polo (who was Nicolo's son and Maffeo's nephew). Marco became a great favorite of Kublai Khan and stayed in China till 1292. He even became the ruler of one of Kublai Khan's largest cities, Hangchow.

Before he returned, Marco Polo had learned of many of the Chinese ports, and because of Chinese trade to the west across the Indian Ocean, he knew of East Africa as far as Zanzibar. He also knew of the Spice Islands and Japan. When he returned to his home city of Venice he brought enviable new knowledge with him, about gunpowder, paper and paper money, coal, tea making, and the role of worms that create silk! While captured by Genoese forces, he dictated an account of his amazing adventures, which included vast amounts of new information, not only about China, but about the geography of nearly half of the globe. This is one hallmark of great explorers. How much did they contribute to the world's body of knowledge? These earlier inquisitive explorers were important members of a culture of science that stemmed from world trade and genuine curiosity. For the Polos, crossing over deserts, mountains and very dangerous tribal-dominated countries or regions, theirs was a hard-won knowledge. As you read about Marco Polo's travels, try and count the many new things and descriptions he brought to Mediterranean countries.

Besides the Polos, however, there were many Islamic traders who traveled to China, like Ibn Battuta, who came from Morocco in Northwest Africa. An Italian Jewish rabbi-trader, Jacob d'Ancona, made his way via India in 1270 to the great Chinese trading port of Zaitun, where he spent much of his time. Both of these explorer-travelers left extensive reports of their expeditions, which rivaled those of the Polos but were less known, as are the neglected accounts of Roman Catholic friars who entered China, one of whom became bishop of Zaitun.[2]

In 1453, the Turkish Empire cut off the Silk Road to Asia. But Turkey was thwarted when, in 1497 and 1498, the Portuguese captain Vasco da Gama sailed from Lisbon around the tip of Africa, up to Arab-controlled Mozambique, and across the

Indian Ocean to Calicut on the western coast of India. He faced the hostility of Arab traders who virtually dominated Calicut. He took care of this problem on a second voyage in 1502 with 20 ships to safeguard the interests of colonists brought to India by another Portuguese captain, Pedro Álvares Cabral. Da Gama laid siege to Calicut and destroyed a fleet of 29 warships. He secured Calicut for the Portuguese settlers and opened a spice route to the islands of the Indies that made Portugal and Spain rich. Spices were valued nearly as much as gold since without refrigeration, foods would spoil. The spices disguised this, and also made the food taste good. Virtually every culture in the world has some kind of stew. Almost all of them depend on spices. Can you name some spices that come from the faraway Spice Islands?

Of course most Americans have heard of Christopher Columbus, who in 1492 sailed west across the Atlantic for the Indies and China. Instead, on four voyages, he reached Hispaniola (now Haiti and the Dominican Republic), Cuba and Jamaica. He created a vision of a New World, populated by what he misleadingly called Indians.

Conquistadors like the Italian sailing for Portugal, Amerigo Vespucci, followed Columbus and in 1502 reached South America at what is now Brazil. His landing there explains Brazil's Portuguese language origins as well as how America got its name on Renaissance charts drawn on vellum or dried sheepskin.

Meanwhile, the English heard of a Portuguese discovery of marvelous fishing grounds off Labrador (discovered by the Vikings and rediscovered by a mysterious freelance Portuguese sailor named the "Labrador"). They sent John Cabot in 1497 to locate these fishing grounds. He found them, and Newfoundland and Labrador as well. It marked the British discovery of North America.

In this first series there are strange tales of other explorers of new lands—Juan Ponce de León, who sought riches and possibly a fountain of youth (everlasting life) and died in Florida; Francisco Coronado, whose men discovered the Grand Canyon and at Zuñi established what became the heart of the Spanish Southwest before the creation of Santa Fe; and de Soto, who after helping to conquer the Incas, boldly ravaged what is now the

American South and Southeast. He also found that the Indian Mound Builder cultures, centered in Cahokia across the Mississippi from present-day St. Louis, had no gold and did not welcome him. Garcilaso de la Vega, the last Inca, lived to write de Soto's story, called *The Florida of the Inca*—a revenge story to match that of Cervantes, who like Garcilaso de la Vega ended up in the tiny Spanish town of Burgos. The two writers never met. Why was this—especially since Cervantes was the tax collector? Perhaps this was when he was in prison writing *Don Quixote*.

In 1513 Vasco Núñez de Balboa discovered the Pacific Ocean "from a peak in Darien"[3] and was soon beheaded by a rival conquistador. But perhaps the greatest Pacific feat was Ferdinand Magellan's voyage around the world from 1519 to 1522, which he did not survive.

Magellan was a Portuguese who sailed for Spain down the Atlantic and through the Strait of Magellan—a narrow passage to the Pacific. He journeyed across that ocean to the Philippines, where he was killed in a fight with the natives. As a recent biography put it, he had "sailed over the edge of the world."[4] His men continued west, and the *Victoria,* the last of his five ships, worn and battered, reached Spain.

Sir Francis Drake, a privateer and lifelong enemy of Spain, sailed for Queen Elizabeth of England on a secret mission in 1577 to find a passage across the Americas for England. Though he sailed, as he put it, "along the backside of Nueva Espanola"[5] as far north as Alaska perhaps, he found no such passage. He then sailed west around the world to England. He survived to help defeat the huge Spanish Armada sent by Phillip II to take England in 1588. Alas he could not give up his bad habit of privateering, and died of dysentery off Porto Bello, Panama. Drake did not find what he was looking for "beyond the ranges," but it wasn't his curiosity that killed him. He may have been the greatest explorer of them all!

While reading our series of great explorers, think about the many questions that arise in your reading, which I hope inspires you to great deeds.

Notes

1. Rudyard Kipling, "The Explorer" (1898). See Jon Heurtl, *Rudyard Kipling: Selected Poems* (New York: Barnes & Noble Books, 2004), 7.

2. Jacob D'Ancona, David Shelbourne, translator, *The City of Light: The Hidden Journal of the Man Who Entered China Four Years Before Marco Polo* (New York: Citadel Press, 1997).

3. John Keats, "On First Looking Into Chapman's Homer."

4. Laurence Bergreen, *Over the Edge of the World: Magellan's Terrifying Circumnavigation of the Globe* (New York: William Morrow & Company, 2003).

5. See Richard Hakluyt, *Principal Navigations, Voyages, Traffiques and Discoveries of the English Nation*; section on Sir Francis Drake.

Conquering
an Empire

It was one of the boldest moves of the sixteenth century—to enter an unknown country with 168 soldiers. But gold was a hypnotic lure, and the two Spanish explorers seeking treasure in Peru—Hernando de Soto and Francisco Pizarro—were not about to turn around and leave the glory to someone else. What they did not know as they started to make their way deep into the country was that they would be discovering the Inca Empire, a highly developed civilization for that time.

Pizarro had authority over Hernando de Soto because five years earlier, he had been the first to enter Peru. He had seen enough of the treasures in the southern city of Tumbez to rush back to Spain and ask King Charles I to give him the concession to Peru. Explorers needed the king's permission to conquer a country.

Hernando de Soto was already a wealthy man living in Nicaragua, but he was first and foremost a *conquistador*, which means conqueror in Spanish. Pizarro had wanted de Soto to join his expedition because he could supply its ships and because he had a reputation as an expert horseman and fighter.

As Pizarro and de Soto pushed through the dense foliage in an area of Tahuantinsuyu, which is what the Inca called their empire, the two men dreamed of riches that might equal the Aztec Empire in Mexico. That empire had been discovered more than a decade earlier by another Spanish explorer, Hernándo Cortés. Tahuantinsuyu stretched from what is present-day southwestern Colombia to the Rio Maule in southern Chile, and from the city of Tumbez in Peru to Bolivia.[1] It was a world empire that was second in size only to the Ottoman Empire, which covered parts of Asia, Europe and Africa.

When Pizarro and de Soto entered Tumbez, they were shocked to see a city gone to ruin. Bodies were hanging from trees. They were correct in thinking that a civil war was in progress. What they did not know until much later was that the Inca ruler Huayna Capac had died from disease in 1525. He left two sons who were half-brothers—Atahualpa in the north and Huáscar in the south—and each declared himself to be the new ruler of the empire. As Pizarro and his soldiers made their way down the Pacific Coast six years later in 1531, Atahualpa had already captured Huáscar and put him in prison.[2]

A WONDROUS SOCIETY

When the conquistadors came to a crossroads, Pizarro divided the soldiers and sent de Soto and his men to a majestic city of temples and palaces called Cajas. Here, de Soto realized that the

Spaniards had happened upon an intelligent and sophisticated society. The Inca Highway that lay before him was an engineering feat. Over 10,000 miles of pavement connected towns in the empire.[3] The Inca stonemasons were artists whose stones fit together perfectly without the use of mortar. Their contributions in the fields of astronomy, medicine, and horticulture were obvious. On the other hand, de Soto learned that the people were ruled with an iron fist. They were told which gods to worship and even what to wear.

De Soto, now on his own, ignored Pizarro's commands to leave the people alone. He entered a sacred temple with his men. Five hundred young women were inside. The Spanish soldiers assaulted them. The people of Cajas were furious and tried to fight the raiders, but were unsuccessful. De Soto, having no remorse, took his small troop to another Inca city called Sana, where Pizarro was waiting.

Atahualpa was in Cajamarca in the southeast. He had sent spies to observe the strangers as they made their way through the foothills of the Andes Mountains. He sent an envoy to invite them to meet him. He could not imagine that so few men could be harmful. The small battalion of men wearing fancy clothes looked ridiculous next to the Inca army of 200,000 men.[4]

The Spaniards were worried that they were entering a trap, but they decided to continue on. When they came to a hill that overlooked Cajamarca, they saw below the largest army any of them had ever imagined. It consisted of 40,000 to 80,000 men. This was not even the main army of the Inca Empire, but instead was an escort for Atahualpa. The Spaniards knew that if they showed the fear they were feeling, they would be killed. Pizarro ordered the men to enter with their flags and banners waving and to strap on every weapon and ornament they had to try to create an impression of strength. Much to their shock, the Incas, instead of attacking, sent food to them. The Spaniards wondered if they were being poisoned.

De Soto was known for his determination to be first. He offered to meet with Atahualpa. Pizarro and his brothers rode with him to the gate. Atahualpa and de Soto were both about the same age. The Inca leader was around "thirty years old, good-looking, somewhat stout, with a fine face, handsome and

When Hernando de Soto met with Atahualpa, the Inca ruler, for the first time, he showed off his skills on a horse. His performance amazed the Incas, who were not familiar with the animals.

fierce, the eyes bloodshot."[5] When de Soto rode up to him wearing his finery and polished armor and weapons, the Inca stared at the ground, ignoring him. De Soto told him that the intentions of the Spaniards were friendly. He invited the ruler to visit Pizarro in Cajamarca the following day.

Suddenly, de Soto asked that one of his spirited horses be brought in. He performed a show, which amazed the Incas, who were not familiar with horses. Afterward, the Spanish soldiers were led to a place where they could sleep. They stayed awake all night, figuring out their next plan of action. They knew from what they had seen on their journey inland that the Incas, for all their politeness, could be vicious.

CONFRONTING ATAHUALPA

They came up with a simple plan. Most of the soldiers would hide in buildings surrounding the plaza in Cajamarca. Pizarro and de Soto would invite Atahualpa to dinner. Starting late on November 16, 1532, Atahualpa began a slow four-mile journey to Cajamarca, where the Spanish awaited him. The 5,000 to 6,000 soldiers with him were unarmed except for axes and slings.

A member of the Spanish expedition, a priest, invited Atahualpa to dinner, and he said no. The priest began to lecture him, and Atahualpa threw the Bible the priest had handed him onto the floor. The Spanish soldiers ran out yelling "*Santiago*"

("St. James," the patron saint of Spain), and the Spanish artillerymen fired at the Incas.[6]

The Incas had never heard the booming noise of cannons, and they were further shocked when they saw some of their men on the ground, killed by the Spanish weapons. Before they could regain their composure, a trumpet roared, and the rest of the soldiers came screaming out and smashed into the crowd of Incas. Blood ran everywhere as the Spaniards started slaughtering the Incas.

Atahualpa was watching from above, for his servants had lifted his litter, or royal chair, up above their heads. The Spanish soldiers killed the servants, and were about to murder Atahualpa when Pizarro stepped in and saved him. The soldiers continued slaughtering the natives. At the end of the attack, they had killed around 8,000 people. Governors, nobles, generals, and priests of the Inca Empire were among those dead.

The victory shocked the Spaniards almost as much as it shocked Atahualpa. But the ruler remembered something. Seven years before, when Spaniards had first arrived in their strange dress, Atahualpa's father had warned that if they returned it would be

Francisco Pizarro takes Atahualpa prisoner. In the battle to capture Atahualpa, a small band of Spanish soldiers killed thousands of Incas. Among the dead were Inca governors, nobles, and priests.

the end of the empire. He was too late remembering his father's words.

For Hernando de Soto, the slaughter of the Incas felt like his finest hour. It remained to be seen where this success would take him.

Test Your Knowledge

1 Why was Francisco Pizarro so eager to have Hernando de Soto join his expedition to Peru?
   a. Because de Soto had a reputation as an expert horseman
   b. Because of de Soto's fighting skills
   c. Because de Soto could supply the expedition's ships
   d. All of the above

2 How were the Spaniards met by the Incas at Cajamarca?
   a. The Incas sent a small troop of men to test the Spaniards' fighting skills.
   b. The Incas sent food to the Spaniards.
   c. The Incas attacked the Spaniards with the full force of their army.
   d. None of the above.

3 How did de Soto attempt to impress the Incas and their leader Atahualpa?
   a. With a display of horsemanship
   b. With gifts of shell necklaces and Spanish cloth
   c. With a demonstration of Spanish cannons
   d. None of the above

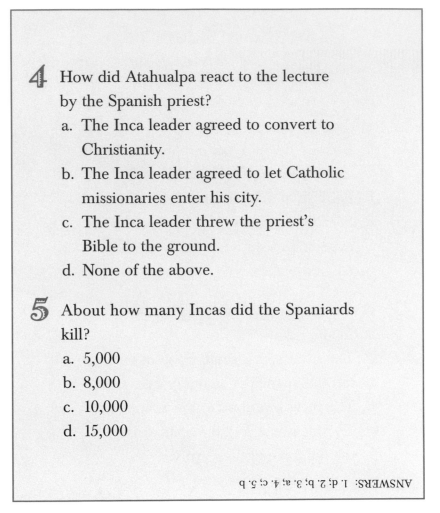

4 How did Atahualpa react to the lecture
by the Spanish priest?

   a. The Inca leader agreed to convert to
      Christianity.

   b. The Inca leader agreed to let Catholic
      missionaries enter his city.

   c. The Inca leader threw the priest's
      Bible to the ground.

   d. None of the above.

5 About how many Incas did the Spaniards
kill?

   a. 5,000

   b. 8,000

   c. 10,000

   d. 15,000

ANSWERS: 1. d; 2. b; 3. a; 4. c; 5. b

The Boy Adventurer

Hernando de Soto's surname was actually Soto,[7] but here he will be referred to as the more familiar de Soto. He was born around 1500 in Jerez de los Caballeros in the Spanish province of Estremadura. The province was the land of the conquistadors. One-half of those who sailed to the Indies during de Soto's lifetime

A bridge from the Roman days still stands in the rugged countryside of the Estremadura region of Spain. The province was the birthplace of many of Spain's conquistadors, including de Soto.

were from Estremadura. Even today, the desolate and harsh landscape breeds people who are small, practical, and tough.[8] Fighting was a way of life for the conquistadors. They had been at war with the Muslims in Spain for centuries, and they were used to winning through their military daring.

Historians are uncertain whether Hernando's parents, Francisco Mendez Soto and Leonor Arias

Tinoco, were poor or of noble birth. But because their son had to borrow money to make his first voyage, it is perhaps safe to place the family in the middle between poverty and nobility. De Soto had three brothers. Life wasn't easy for families during those years. They lived in walled towns, and the world beyond was considered unsafe. Boys in the village liked to play games that involved swordplay. Reports about the adventures of Christopher Columbus in the New World in 1492 carried to the most distant villages, and it is easy to imagine that Hernando de Soto dreamed at a young age of following in his footsteps.

SETTLEMENTS IN THE NEW WORLD

Columbus had taken 1,200 settlers to found Santo Domingo, Europe's first permanent settlement in the Western Hemisphere. In 1502, a second settlement of 2,500 people was created there. Once the settlements had been established, it became fairly easy to conquer Puerto Rico, Cuba, and the mainland, then called Tierra Firme (modern-day Panama).

King Ferdinand II, who, with his wife, Isabella, ruled Spain, supported all of these conquests. Like most Spaniards of that era, he believed that God had called them to rule the Indies. They were to convert the natives of those lands to Christianity and to spread the Spanish culture. Finally, and perhaps most important, the king and his conquistadors were obsessed with gold and expanding their empire.

However, in the early 1500s, the explorers' reports to the king told of warfare with the natives and outbreaks of disease. This made the king hesitant to send another fleet of ships. Supporting the explorers was expensive for the government, especially when the results were uncertain.

But then an adventurer named Vasco Núñez de Balboa wrote to the king about a "southern sea" he had been told about that was only a few days' march south of Santa Maria in Tierra Firme. Not long after that, Balboa discovered the Pacific Ocean. The king had thought Balboa was long dead, and so those letters arriving in 1511 and 1512 restored Ferdinand's enthusiasm for future conquests. For years he had dreamed of an ideal colony that would incorporate Catholic values, that would make a profit, and that would not cost the government too much.

A letter from Vasco Núñez de Balboa, above, to King Ferdinand of Spain describing a "southern sea" helped spur a new Spanish voyage to Panama. In 1513, Balboa discovered the Pacific Ocean.

Around the same time, in 1513, Juan Ponce de León visited what he believed to be an island north of Cuba and named it *La Florida,* or land of flowers.[9] He was probably sailing up the eastern coastline, south of present-day Jacksonville.

Back in Spain, rumors of a voyage to Panama spread across the country. A man named Pedrarias Dávila was appointed captain and governor of the new colony. The 70-year-old Dávila was a cruel soldier who had fought in many wars. The king spared no expense for this expedition, even when it threw his country into debt. By the time the 18 ships were ready to sail, 2,000 settlers had signed up.

A TEENAGE VOYAGER

It is easy to imagine the 14-year-old Hernando de Soto, with a sword and buckler strapped to him, wearing big boots, responding to the call. He was probably with an adult, a nobleman perhaps, or a local captain. Once in Seville, Spain, potential passengers had to wait in long lines to be interviewed by senior officers. They were asked their names and ages, and were questioned about their military experience. One of the boys with de Soto was Hernán Ponce de León (not Juan Ponce de León, who named La Florida), who would become a close friend and business partner.

Many of the colonists had to pay high fares to go. The richest people took their slaves, horses, and fine clothing. Pedrarias Dávila had even persuaded the king to hire bands and set off fireworks at the grand farewell party. As the travelers made their way through the streets of Seville, waving to families and onlookers, it seemed as if nothing could go wrong. But when they arrived at the docks, they realized that there was not enough room for everyone. The expedition was delayed, but finally, after six weeks, everyone gathered again at the docks. It was February 25, 1514.

The fleet sailed down the coast. Soon it ran into a storm that damaged some ships and threatened to halt the expedition. Everyone was forced to stay in a small village, where Pedrarias Dávila took bribe money and added more passengers to the crowded ships. Soon, the fleet headed to the Canary Islands— sailing the same route to the island of Dominica that Columbus took on his second voyage.

(continued on page 22)

The Spanish Empire

What is referred to as the Spanish Empire is the conquered colonies, territory, and resources that fell under the rule of Spain's kings from the late fifteenth century through the sixteenth century. The expansion started with Christopher Columbus, who on his first voyage landed on Hispaniola, the island that today is the Dominican Republic and Haiti. Those areas were named the Indies because Columbus thought he was in the East Indies. That is how the people in the Caribbean and the Americas came to be called Indians.

Columbus made three more trips from 1493 to 1502. Other Spanish explorers made their way through Central and South America, claiming the territory and the people they conquered for Spain. The conquests increased Spain's wealth and power vastly. The Catholic Church also gained from Spanish imperialism, for the colonists who settled the new lands carried their religion with them.

In 1516, Charles I took the throne in Spain. He already ruled what is now Belgium and the Netherlands. Three years later he became emperor of the Holy Roman Empire as Charles V, which meant he ruled the Western Empire, except for Britain. Then, Hernándo Cortés went into Mexico

and in 1521 conquered the Aztec Empire, which
was added to the Spanish Empire. In the 1530s,
Francisco Pizarro and Hernando de Soto conquered
the Inca Empire in Peru. Expeditions pushed
farther north into Ecuador and Colombia and south
into Chile. The conquistadors were unstoppable.
They went into Argentina in 1536 and founded
the city of Buenos Aires, and continued on into
Paraguay in 1537. Most of the South American
continent, Central America, Mexico, Florida
(which included most of North America in the
Spaniards' minds), and Cuba were all under
control of the Spanish Empire in the 1550s.

Spain tried to remain in charge of all commerce
within the empire, but in the 1520s England,
France, and the Netherlands were starting to
enter Spanish territories. It wasn't until the late
1500s, however, that Europeans started fighting
for commerce and international power. After
1620 Spain lost a lot of its imperial, commercial
and economic control over its colonies. Spain's
power remained dominant, though, until the late
1700s. Then the colonies began fighting for their
independence. But the Spanish influence had and
has been enormous.

(continued from page 19)

De Soto would have been traveling as a simple soldier or perhaps a page. Because of his lowly status, he would have been jammed below the decks for most of the voyage, sleeping among dozens of other men and various animals, including horses. On June 2, the fleet reached Dominica, where everyone rejoiced to be on land again, even if only for a few days. As the expedition was leaving, Pedrarias Dávila became furious with a crewman who had gotten drunk. He ordered him to come onboard, and when the crewman did not obey, Dávila had him hung from a tree in view of everyone on the ships.[10]

Hernando de Soto was becoming thoroughly initiated in the world of the conquistador. The driving philosophy of the conquistador—that he had to win at all costs—would play a major role in his future development. And Pedrarias Dávila, who would live to be 90, would be a shadow in de Soto's life for many years to come.

Test Your Knowledge

1 De Soto's boyhood region of Estremadura was known for

a. its silk.

b. its gold.

c. its dry climate.

d. all of the above.

2 Why did the Spaniards of 1500 feel it essential to travel to the Americas?

a. To convert the natives to Christianity

b. To secure gold and treasure for Spain

c. To bring slaves back to Spain

d. a and b only

3 What was Vasco Núñez de Balboa's great discovery?

a. Gold in Peru

b. The Pacific Ocean

c. The Panama Canal

d. None of the above

4 De Soto made his first sea voyage at the age of 14. What was the voyage's intended destination?

a. Panama

b. Peru

c. Mexico

d. Florida

5 What was the driving philosophy of the conquistador?

   a. To show compassion and mercy to those he
      conquered
   b. To win at any and all costs
   c. To convert all he conquered to Christianity
   d. None of the above

ANSWERS: 1. c; 2. d; 3. b; 4. a; 5. b

Conquering Nicaragua

The evil Pedrarias Dávila locked up the food supplies soon after he landed with the settlers. Disease broke out, killing many of them. Dávila was now insanely jealous of another explorer, Vasco Núñez de Balboa, who discovered the Pacific Ocean. When King Ferdinand died, Charles I became the king of Spain in 1516. He decided to replace Dávila. The governor was furious, and began accusing Balboa of many crimes. A brief trial followed, and Balboa was beheaded in 1519. Dávila went so far as to have his head put on a pole and left in the middle of town.[11]

Little is known of de Soto's activities until he was around 20. He quickly went from being a simple soldier to a senior captain and conquistador. Dávila continued on as leader of the colonists, and it is believed that de Soto was sent on expeditions and raids on a regular basis, developing the skills that would later make him famous. Around age 20, de Soto met Francisco Pizarro for the first time. He was placed under Pizarro's command, and together they organized a raid on an Indian village called Nata in Panama. It turned out to be successful.

From 1519 to the end of 1523, de Soto established a home base in Nata, acquiring gold and Indian slaves through many expeditions. Dávila had ordered his men to settle this land. They were to use the Indians they captured to build their houses and farm their land. The Indians, who were fearful of the Spaniards, were forced to hunt and fish for their new owners, as well as perform any other work they were

The Sambu River in Darien, Panama, is pictured here at dusk. From 1519 to 1523, Hernando de Soto made his home in Nata, Panama. There, on several expeditions, he acquired gold and Indian slaves.

called upon to do. It was the beginning of a massive slave operation that would continue for many years. The conquistadors, who numbered 50 to 60, demanded a workforce of thousands because they wanted to be treated like royalty. They had been given the chance to develop a taste for the independence and excitement of frontier life. They felt above the law.

(continued on page 30)

Slavery

The Spaniards said they believed in a just war, but their actions often belied their words. Queen Isabella, in 1500, outlawed slavery, unless the Indians attacked Spanish soldiers or there was proof that they were cannibals. The conquistadors knew how to get around such rules.

The Spanish were under the strict rules of the Catholic Church. When they came across Indians who were cannibals, or who got drunk, or who behaved in strange ways, the Spaniards believed that they were under the spell of Satan. They were thought of as beasts. In 1542, the royalty issued another decree forbidding the Spanish to take slaves. But de Soto and others had long been operating a slave market from Central America.

At first, de Soto and his partners forced their captured Indians to work in the mines in the mountain region of Nicaragua. The work was brutal, and many died. The first of their documented slave ships departed Nicaragua for Panama in March 1529. The ships could carry 450 slaves. De Soto and his partner Hernán Ponce de León made a large profit with the slaves. They sold a beautiful woman or a very strong man for 2 to 12 pesos. (The average sailor earned 16 or 17 pesos per year.) From 1524 to 1549, 500,000 Indians were captured and either died on ships, in the mines, committed suicide, or became ill.*

Even before Nicaragua, Spaniards went out looking for people to kidnap into slavery. A captain named Pedro de Salazar sailed from Hispaniola around 1514 to capture slaves in the Bahamas. Later, he sailed up to the coast of South Carolina and captured Indians who were larger than average. He took them back to Hispaniola.

Things changed slightly when de Soto entered La Florida. The Indians there fought back more than the Nicaraguans or the Incas had done. In the great Battle of Mabila, which occurred toward the end of de Soto's expedition, all of the Indian porters whom the Spaniards had with them ran to join the Indians. That move was the beginning of the end for de Soto.

* Duncan, David Ewing, *Hernando de Soto: A Savage Quest in the Americas* (Norman, OK: University of Oklahoma Press, 1996), 101.

(continued from page 27)

In 1520 Hernando de Soto heard of a man named Hernándo Cortés, who had discovered the Aztec Empire in Mexico. He had kidnapped the emperor Moctezuma in broad daylight. De Soto heard the rumors of exotic cities and mountains of gold. This surely whetted his appetite for more adventure.

In 1523, another explorer, Gil González Dávila, sailed up to the beach of Panama carrying 112,000 pesos worth of gold. He told of a country as rich as Mexico, which he mispronounced, calling it Nicaragua. The actual name was Nic-atl-nahuac. After Gil González Dávila had returned to Santo Domingo and spent most of his money, he decided to try again to conquer the kingdom of Nic-atl-nahuac. Governor Pedrarias Dávila considered the man with the same surname his rival.

Pedrarias Dávila held the order from King Charles to conquer Nicaragua. He appointed a soldier named Francisco Hernández de Córdoba to be the captain of the Governor's Guard. There were too many men who wanted to be the first to conquer Nicaragua. Cortés, who had conquered Mexico, was one. And Gil González Dávila was another.

INVASION OF NICARAGUA

Córdoba was put in charge of Governor Dávila's soldiers waiting to invade Nicaragua. De Soto signed on as commander of one of the marching companies. A man named Bartolomé de Las Casas, who had visited Nicaragua during the 1520s, called it a "paradise of God" with its magnificent freshwater lake the size of the Chesapeake Bay and its numerous volcanoes.[12] But Córdoba and de Soto were much more interested in finding gold.

The natives of Nicaragua had originated in Mexico, and at the time of de Soto's invasion, about 500,000 Indians were living there. Córdoba, with his 230-man army, headed for the coast of Costa Rica, south of Nicaragua. No records exist of what happened next. It is likely that Córdoba marched into Nicaragua, with de Soto in front of the lead battalion as usual. De Soto and his men surged across the Great Valley, fighting some powerful armies. It is surprising that the natives gave in within a few weeks of the Spanish invasion. One reason may be that the Nicaraguan style of warfare was more one-on-one, with a great deal of ceremony involved in the preparation for battle. Though the conquistadors were not in great shape, they were still superior to the Indians when it came to war tactics.

Córdoba then started doing what he liked best—building towns and creating a new government. He was not as much of a warrior as his comrades were. He founded Granada, and then settled León, laying out plans for plazas, churches and public buildings. He also built defenses against the rebel Indians, and rival Spanish captains.

Córdoba sent one of his men on a scouting expedition. He came across Gil González Dávila, who had an army with him. Gil González was quite unhappy about meeting up with one of Pedrarias Dávila's conquistadors, and sent a message to Córdoba that he had no business on that land. Córdoba sent Hernando de Soto to let Gil González Dávila know that Nicaragua was already taken.

DE SOTO HUMILIATED

Gil González Dávila had already made a fortune from the gold he had found earlier in Nicaragua. He had as much power as de Soto. He was also more cunning. Keeping up with de Soto's progress toward his camp, he made a surprise attack on de Soto and his 80 soldiers while they were sleeping. De Soto rallied his men to fight back, however, and overcame González Dávila, who pretended to be sorry. De Soto fell for his words, and let the matter rest, only to be attacked again by the determined González Dávila.

This time de Soto was taken prisoner, and his gold was stolen. Though de Soto was humiliated, no one was hurt, as González Dávila knew that Córdoba was nearby. He decided to release de Soto and his men and return to Honduras. Córdoba, when he learned what had happened, was relieved rather than upset with de Soto, and he rewarded de Soto handsomely for his work.

Córdoba's next action was to ask the king to make Nicaragua a colony, and with this in mind, he drew up a letter. He wanted to be governor. Rumors had spread to Pedrarias Dávila that Córdoba had met with Hernándo Cortés early during his conquest of Nicaragua to discuss teaming up against Pedrarias Dávila. Hernando de Soto shocked Córdoba by publicly accusing Córdoba of disloyalty to Pedrarias Dávila. He claimed that he knew about the meeting between Córdoba and Cortés.

A Nicaraguan archaeologist examines the tomb of Francisco Hernández de Córdoba, who helped conquer Nicaragua. De Soto served with Córdoba, and then later betrayed him.

An angry Córdoba threw de Soto in jail. De Soto's friend and business partner, Francisco Companon, rescued him, and they took off. Córdoba chased them. When he caught up to them, de Soto stood his ground. He knew that Córdoba would back down from a fight. He threatened to hack Córdoba to pieces. Córdoba called off the attack, which turned out to be a mistake.[13]

When Pedrarias Dávila came after him, Córdoba explained that he had never intended to revolt and begged Dávila to believe him. He begged for mercy. But the cold-blooded Governor Dávila, at age 84, had not changed. He ordered Córdoba beheaded. Once again, Hernando de Soto was witness to the extreme cruelty of the man who had led him to Central America. Only this time, de Soto was the cause of the victim's death. Most believe he acted for his own gain. Without Córdoba in the picture, he had a chance of becoming the governor of Nicaragua. This would not be the last time that de Soto would put someone's life in danger for his own advancement.

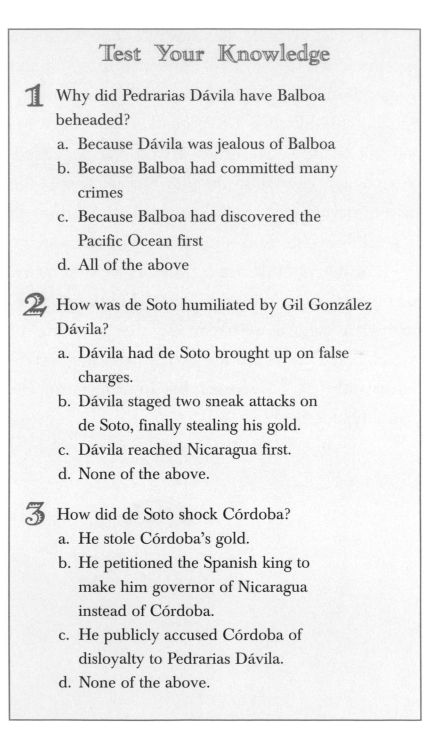

Test Your Knowledge

1 Why did Pedrarias Dávila have Balboa beheaded?
   a. Because Dávila was jealous of Balboa
   b. Because Balboa had committed many crimes
   c. Because Balboa had discovered the Pacific Ocean first
   d. All of the above

2 How was de Soto humiliated by Gil González Dávila?
   a. Dávila had de Soto brought up on false charges.
   b. Dávila staged two sneak attacks on de Soto, finally stealing his gold.
   c. Dávila reached Nicaragua first.
   d. None of the above.

3 How did de Soto shock Córdoba?
   a. He stole Córdoba's gold.
   b. He petitioned the Spanish king to make him governor of Nicaragua instead of Córdoba.
   c. He publicly accused Córdoba of disloyalty to Pedrarias Dávila.
   d. None of the above.

4 How did Pedrarias Dávila deal with the accusations against Córdoba?

a. He offered Córdoba a full pardon, provided he return to Spain.

b. He had Córdoba beheaded.

c. He retired and allowed Córdoba to become governor.

d. None of the above.

5 Why do most current sources believe de Soto sabotaged Córdoba?

a. Because de Soto stood to gain from Córdoba's absence

b. Because de Soto truly feared a rebellion by Córdoba

c. Because de Soto wrongly believed Córdoba to be a traitor

d. None of the above

ANSWERS: 1. a; 2. b; 3. c; 4. b; 5. a

The Central America Years

King Charles I appointed a man named Diego López de Salcedo to be the first governor of Honduras. But even sending one of his own men did not give the king much control over the captains in Central America. They were too far away to control, and they knew it.

Pedrarias Dávila was hated, but the local settlers were too afraid of his power to say anything. When he left to go back to Spain to meet with the king, all the Spaniards in Central America hoped they had seen the last of him. He had committed many crimes during his governorship, and some wished he would be tried and punished once he was back in Spain.

A NEW LEADER

Diego López de Salcedo arrived in Trujillo, Honduras, in 1527, soon after Dávila had departed. He looked around and was not impressed with the small, dusty capital. As soon as he was settled, he set up an expedition to the richer lands south of him. He and a battalion of 150 men on horseback went on a killing spree that took them down the mountain highways of Honduras. They killed as many Indians as they could. They also captured Indians for their slave operation. This angered the natives, who began attacking the Europeans, driving most of them into the cities of León and Granada in Nicaragua. The citizens had no choice but to recognize Salcedo as their new governor.

De Soto and his friends and business partners, Francisco Companon and Hernán Ponce de León, decided to support Salcedo. For one thing, he allowed the shipment of slaves from Nicaragua to Panama. De Soto was immediately put in charge of an army sent out to crush the rebelling Indians in the north. Later, he was named the captain of the Governor's Guard, which gave him much more power. He had been in Central America long enough to know how to terrorize the Indians by capturing them and torturing or hanging them, but he added his own method for "pacifying" them. De Soto would bring out treaties after he had terrorized and tortured the natives, and he would force the rebel leaders to swear obedience to him in exchange for their lives.

The peace that followed was short-lived, for King Charles sent the old devil Pedrarias Dávila back to Central America as the first legal governor of the new colony of Nicaragua. This left out Salcedo, who was infuriated. The king also appointed Francisco de Castañeda, a man known for being shrewd and ruthless at court, as the royal mayor. One of his duties would be to keep Dávila in check.

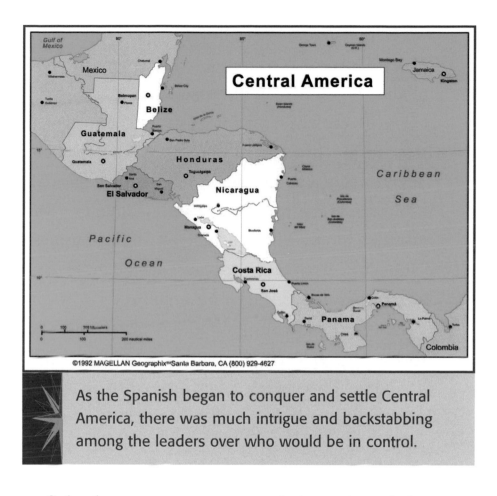

As the Spanish began to conquer and settle Central America, there was much intrigue and backstabbing among the leaders over who would be in control.

Salcedo was so angry over being rejected that he sent some of his men to destroy the city of Bruselas, where Dávila was due to arrive. That move caused the council in León—led by Hernando de Soto—to throw him in prison. Once again, de Soto jumped in to betray a superior who had once bestowed honors and wealth on him. Salcedo was forced to pay a high ransom for his own life. He was in prison for a year, but died soon after being released, probably from the treatment he received in jail.

Dávila, now almost 90 years old, returned to León to much celebration and fanfare. De Soto, only 28 years old, decided to stay in Nicaragua. He would spend the next few years building up a vast business empire, which included a mining business, a shipping business, and a slave operation. He and his two partners, Companon and Ponce de León, had under their control thousands of Indian slaves working as farmers, servants, and miners.[14] The real money in Central America lay in kidnapping Indians from rural areas and marching them to León, where they were shipped off to Panama or sent to work in the mines.

CRUELTY

De Soto and the other Spaniards were shockingly cruel to the natives of Central America. Thousands of slaves were sent to the mountains to mine for gold. Many died from starvation, weather conditions, or overwork. When they became exhausted, they were killed.[15]

The conquistadors were frontiersmen, and while their lives were often in danger as they traveled to rural villages seeking gold and slaves, the degree of savagery they exhibited can never be justified. Fear played a big part, as the number of conquerors was quite small compared with the large population of Indians they were trying to control and change. But even fear doesn't explain the suffering and torture the natives underwent. Nicaragua was basically a lawless country, where those in control could do as they pleased and never suffer consequences.

One thing the conquistadors could not control was disease. A plague occurred in Nicaragua in the 1520s that left a huge impact on de Soto. Francisco Companon was one of the first to die when a fever struck the mines, killing vast numbers of Indians and Spaniards alike. His death was a great loss to de Soto, who considered him his closest friend.

De Soto moved to León with his companion, Juana Hernandez, where they were surrounded by all the luxuries available. They lived in an adobe structure, a brick and mortar building plastered with clay and whitewashed with pigments from ground shells. There were barns for the horses and vegetable

(continued on page 46)

The Conquistadors

*C*onquistador in Spanish means conqueror.
Hernando de Soto and his fellow conquistadors
were from a warrior caste. Most were probably
hidalgos, which means "sons of someone." * They
had driven the conquering Moors out of Spain.
They were proud, and they went to great lengths,
even as youths, to defend their honor. They believed
in courage, family, loyalty to each other, country,
and one's own name.

No matter how strongly people feel when they
read about the behavior of the conquistadors who
killed off entire populations in their quests for
gold and other treasures, it is important to realize
that their discoveries were a turning point in the
history of the world. People, for the first time,
were learning about the shape and scale of the
Earth. During the sixteenth century, amazing
exploits were achieved. Ferdinand Magellan's
expedition circumnavigated the globe. Hernándo
Cortés overthrew the Aztecs. Francisco Pizarro
and Hernando de Soto conquered the Inca. Their
journeys of exploration are filled with stories of
incredible bravery, cruelty, greed, and endurance.

"The *Conquista* [conquest]," according to the
writer Michael Wood, "was at once one of the

most significant events in history, and one of the most cruel and devastating." **

As an adult, de Soto was skilled in the conquista's strongest weapon: a quick lunge forward deep into enemy territory, then the unexpected charge in the midst of battle. He learned at an early age to master the skills of a horseman and a knight. He was a man of many contradictions. He was destructive, arrogant, and savage. And he was inspiring. Once his riders covered 250 miles in just five days. He was a liar, and he was hot-tempered and competitive. What he craved more than anything else was success.

The conquistadors who explored the world during the 1500s did not seem to know when to stop. Cortés spent his great fortune and ended his life in lawsuits. Pizarro, de Soto's commander in Peru, was killed in Lima by rivals. De Soto risked his own life and the lives of his soldiers by making a decision that involved pride. The conquistadors would fade out in the next century.

* David Ewing Duncan, *Hernando de Soto: A Savage Quest in the Americas* (Norman, OK: University of Oklahoma Press, 1996), 12.

** Michael Wood, "The Story of the Conquistadors," *http://www.bbc.co.uk/history/discovery/exploration/conquistadors_05.shtml*

(continued from page 43)

gardens and fruit trees. He and Juana had a daughter named Maria de Soto.[16]

The political atmosphere in Central America, however, was never calm. Pedrarias Dávila and Francisco de Castañeda, the new royal mayor, started competing for dominance over the area. Because the king appointed him, Castañeda was able to operate independently of any other authority. De Soto and Hernán Ponce de León were on Castañeda's side, and became good friends with him. Again, de Soto sided with the man who would offer him the most.

The rivalry between Castañeda and Dávila never led to either of their deaths. These men realized that there was no point. By this time, all of them were wealthy. Perhaps they enjoyed all the intrigue and competition. It was like being in a high-stakes poker game.

Though de Soto's position in León led him into politics, where he attended many meetings and hearings, he must have found himself longing at times to go on another quest. He did continue making journeys into the wilderness with the goal of pacifying the Indians. But de Soto, along with many

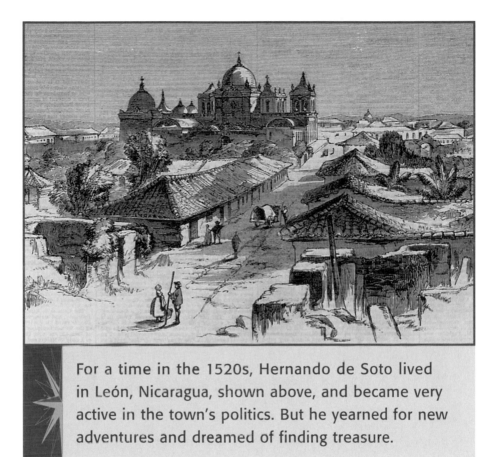

For a time in the 1520s, Hernando de Soto lived in León, Nicaragua, shown above, and became very active in the town's politics. But he yearned for new adventures and dreamed of finding treasure.

others, continued to dream of finding a fairy-tale kingdom of gold somewhere.

A FUTURE CONQUEST

Early in 1527, a group of Spaniards happened upon a rare boat built from reeds and planks and took a few of the passengers prisoner. The Indian passengers wore elaborate jewelry and garments of beautiful embroidery, and carried pieces of silver and gold. The Spaniards were part of a mission to scout the South American coast. The mission was sent by Francisco Pizarro, de Soto's former leader in Panama. The conquistadors taught the captured passengers Spanish. Pizarro wanted to take them back to Peru the next time he invaded their country.

Pizarro was on the verge of giving up on his attempt to find a kingdom of riches when the mysterious boatload of people was found.[17] A few months later, Pizarro and his men came upon their first Inca city, Tumbez, located between Peru and Ecuador, and were impressed with the riches they saw there. This was what Pizarro needed to prove to the Spanish king that there was a new empire to be discovered. When Pizarro returned to Spain to meet with King Charles, the king presented him, a former peasant, with grand honors, and gave him permission to invade Peru. Pizarro thought immediately of Hernando de Soto.

Test Your Knowledge

1. Why did de Soto and his business partners decide to support Salcedo?
   a. Salcedo would allow the shipment of slaves from Nicaragua to Panama.
   b. De Soto believed that Salcedo was on the verge of discovering gold.
   c. Salcedo blackmailed de Soto to gain his support.
   d. None of the above.

2. How did Salcedo react to the return of Pedrarias Dávila?
   a. Salcedo graciously stepped aside.
   b. Salcedo sought to have his men destroy the city of Bruselas.
   c. Salcedo planned to kill Dávila.
   d. We don't know.

3. De Soto's business empire included
   a. a mining operation.
   b. a slave-trading operation.
   c. a shipping business.
   d. all of the above.

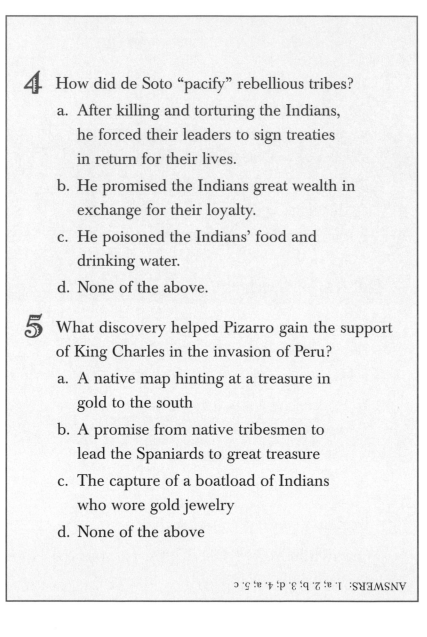

4 How did de Soto "pacify" rebellious tribes?

  a. After killing and torturing the Indians, he forced their leaders to sign treaties in return for their lives.

  b. He promised the Indians great wealth in exchange for their loyalty.

  c. He poisoned the Indians' food and drinking water.

  d. None of the above.

5 What discovery helped Pizarro gain the support of King Charles in the invasion of Peru?

  a. A native map hinting at a treasure in gold to the south

  b. A promise from native tribesmen to lead the Spaniards to great treasure

  c. The capture of a boatload of Indians who wore gold jewelry

  d. None of the above

ANSWERS: 1. a; 2. b; 3. d; 4. a; 5. c

Discovery of Peru

Meanwhile, in the late 1520s, rumors had spread to Nicaragua of a vast empire in the mountains of South America. At the time, Hernando de Soto was deeply involved in local politics. But he had started to investigate the stories. Finding them to have some truth, he, Hernán Ponce de León and Francisco de Castañeda began to make plans to sail in that direction. Everyone knew that the gold originally found in Panama was said to have come from the south. But at de Soto's every attempt to leave, Pedrarias Dávila would step in to stop him.

In 1530, Francisco Pizarro returned from Spain with a formal contract from the king to conquer the land called Peru. This enabled Pizarro to offer men willing to go with him a percentage of the gold and treasure they might find. He wanted Hernando de Soto. Not only did the two men know each other from their years in Panama, but de Soto's reputation as a fearless conqueror and expert horseman was widely known. Pizarro knew that de Soto was a shrewd politician now. He also knew that he was one of the richest men in Central America, and could finance part of the expedition.

Arrangements were secretly made so as not to incite Dávila's anger. De Soto smuggled 30 to 40 Spanish recruits and as many as 300 slaves aboard one of his boats, the *Santiago.* When Dávila became suspicious, de Soto's men prevented Dávila's people from coming aboard by gathering up all the transport craft in the port and beaching them. De Soto

Francisco Pizarro had the contract from the king of Spain to conquer the land called Peru. Pizarro wanted de Soto to join him, because of de Soto's skills as a fighter and because de Soto was wealthy and could help finance the expedition.

continued with his plans and negotiations, ignoring Dávila as much as possible. Dávila then put a ban on anyone leaving the colony. De Soto was furious. Fortunately, for him and everyone concerned, Pedrarias Dávila died on March 6, 1531.

LEAVING FOR A NEW LAND

De Soto and company departed Nicaragua on the *San Geronimo*, the flagship of his slave fleet. He stood on the deck after his farewell ceremony, glittering in the sunlight in his ornate armor, and watched another shore disappear as he set forth on the 1,500-mile voyage to the new land. The ship was filled with men, most of them peasants with various degrees of fighting experience, half of them from Estremadura.

Earlier, Pizarro and his army had gone to Ecuador and suffered many setbacks. They were sick and wounded from a long march and were constantly being attacked by the Puna islanders. When de Soto arrived, they were slowly starving to death. Pizarro, however, after years of trying to conquer Peru, wasn't about to quit. He was known as a second- or third-rate warrior, always in the middle range in terms of skills and intelligence. Now in his 50s, his obsession wasn't as much about ambition for gold as it was about trying to prove himself. He wasn't alone, for he had with him his three half-brothers—Hernando, Juan, and Gonzalo Pizarro—who would later be referred to as the Brothers of Doom. They and de Soto would not get along.

At first, de Soto and his boatload of passengers were elated to meet up finally with Pizarro. Soon, though, they were discouraged when they saw the poor condition of Pizarro's men. De Soto learned that Hernando Pizarro had already named himself lieutenant general, a title that de Soto had insisted on before he left Nicaragua. He at least wanted to be second in command, but it was soon obvious that that was not going to happen. In fact, Pizarro and the others did not want to share power. De Soto was in an odd position. He did not have an independent command, but neither did he think of himself below Pizarro.[18] It all left a bad taste in de Soto's mouth.

With de Soto and his men attached to his expedition, Pizarro counted 300 Spaniards—150 to 200 footmen, and 100 horsemen in his army, far more than Córdoba had had on his expedition. He also had Hernando de Soto, one of the best cavalry officers in the Americas, to lead the horsemen. The importance of such a person cannot be stressed enough, for they were to travel many, many hundreds of miles through a country that was five times the size of Spain, entering the largest and most sophisticated empire in the Western Hemisphere.

CONFLICT WITHIN

Hernando de Soto continued to simmer with rage over Hernando Pizarro being named lieutenant general. His way to deal with the problem was to make sure, as usual, that he was always in front. It was his way of becoming indispensable to Pizarro. The one time he did not go first was when they approached Tumbez, the city Pizarro had entered five years before. The men of Tumbez, led by Quillemesa, came rushing out of the bush and dragged the unsuspecting Spanish soldiers into a nearby forest, where they tortured them and threw them into hot kettles of water.[19]

De Soto went after the Indians, killing all who came across his path. Much to his surprise,

Quillemesa and his men came forward, asked forgiveness for what they had done, and offered peace. Another version of the story, however, says that de Soto fought hard, running up a hill with his horses, and set upon the enemy with such vengeance that they surrendered.

Peru was in the middle of a civil war. This conflict gave the Spanish soldiers an advantage. With two groups of people warring against each other, it was easier for the Spanish to enter Inca territory. Once the Spanish had taken over Cajamarca and had taken the Inca chief, Atahualpa, as a hostage, they were in a position to win the south. The Spanish lancers, mounted on horseback, could kill many people in a short period of time.

Pizarro and de Soto knew, however, that their army was outnumbered 500 to one. Atahualpa was told to tell his soldiers to surrender. Hernando de Soto rode out to the tens of thousands of Inca soldiers; their commanders made the sign of the cross. This indicated that they were surrendering.

Atahualpa, who was also called the Sun King, saw the look of rapture on the faces of the Spanish soldiers after they realized how much gold the Incas

ATAHUALLPA, INCA XIIII.

After Atahualpa's capture, de Soto became friendly with the Inca leader and was somewhat protective of him. De Soto was among the Spaniards who did not want to see Atahualpa executed.

had. He decided to offer them a ransom for his freedom. He took Pizarro into a room and drew a line showing how much gold and silver he was willing to offer for his life. It was equal to the biggest fortunes in Spain. The Spaniards agreed instantly, for they realized that Atahualpa offered them some protection.

They were fascinated by this semi-divine "king" who wore no garment twice, spoke only to the highest born in his land, and when he had to spit, spit into the outstretched hand of a woman.[20] De Soto had conversations with him, and was even a little protective of him.

De Soto was appointed military governor of Cajamarca, and he spent much of his time organiz ing and supervising. In the meantime, he and Pizarro awaited the arrival from Panama of an explorer named Diego de Almagro. He and Pizarro had been partners on earlier expeditions. After two months, he showed up with 153 new soldiers. The lingering question was what to do with the Sun King. Some of the Spaniards wanted to kill him, while others thought to send him into exile in Panama or Spain. All agreed that he would be angry once he learned how dishonest the Spaniards were. They had no intention of letting him go.

THE DEATH OF ATAHUALPA

Rumors reached the Spanish that Atahualpa had gotten word to his generals to attack. No one could sleep. Pizarro had a chain put around his captive's neck. De Soto, among others, thought they did not have the proof they needed to kill the Sun King. Almagro, though, had no patience and demanded that Atahualpa be killed. Pizarro sent de Soto out to investigate whether a vast army was gathering to attack them. While de Soto was away, Pizarro accused his prisoner of treason and had him killed. Some blame Almagro for the murder of the Inca ruler, but no one will ever know exactly what happened.

De Soto returned to announce that there was no danger. Pizarro and the others realized they had made a terrible mistake. De Soto was very critical of Pizarro, and his criticism spread across the Spanish world. Even King Charles condemned the act. Tensions developed among Pizarro, Almagro, and de Soto.

But while they were trying to win a war with the Incas, they could not afford to fight with each other. There was the army in the south that had to be overcome. De Soto almost lost his life by disobeying orders from Pizarro in a major conflict known as the Battle of Vilcaconga. (In the battle, the Incas caught the advance guard, led by de Soto, at dusk after a long march.) But finally the Spaniards could say they had conquered all of Peru when they entered the city of Cuzco on November 15, 1533. Cuzco had a population of 100,000. The people waved and cheered. They were glad to have the civil war over, but they had no idea of the true nature of the men who had just arrived.

The Spaniards moved into the royal palaces, with Hernando de Soto taking the most beautiful. Hundreds of servants took care of his every need. Pizarro made de Soto the lieutenant governor of Cuzco. He was now the second most powerful man in Peru. He brought the most beautiful women in Peru into his harem. De Soto also had a large group of supporters who were very loyal. He knew, however, that his time in Peru was limited because of all the infighting. Diego de Almagro and de Soto were

(continued on page 64)

Treasure

A tahualpa, ruler of the Inca Empire, had
offered Pizarro and de Soto a roomful of
gold and two rooms of silver in exchange for his
life. But neither conquistador was prepared for the
room in Cajamarca that measured 22 feet long by
17 feet wide. The gold started arriving, strapped
to llamas. Some days the Incas would bring in
gold worth the equivalent of 60,000 pesos. There
were cups, earrings, necklaces, and statues, and
solid gold panels arrived from the Temple of the
Sun. Fountains of gold were brought in. At that
point, de Soto ordered the Incas to start melting
everything down. The total ransom equaled
$91 million if measured in today's money.*

One-fifth of the money went to the king of
Spain. The explorers had to decide who got
what amount. De Soto had hoped he would get
the second-largest share after Francisco Pizarro.
But that went instead to Hernando Pizarro. He
received twice what de Soto got. The reality is,
however, that each of them received a huge sum
of money.

Then, when the Spanish soldiers headed
750 miles south to Cuzco from Cajamarca, they
defeated the armies of the southern leaders of the
Inca Empire. The Incas called Cuzco the "Navel of

the World." In the middle of the city were fabulous palaces and mansions. De Soto and his men moved into the palaces. There were fantastic fortunes here, too. The soldiers collected plates, armor, statues, and an array of metal wonders. They put them in storage rooms in Pizarro's palace. They took more gold and silver in Cuzco than they had in Cajamarca.

They found shoes made of gold, and there were golden figures of women, llamas, and all kinds of carved insects. They came upon an entire garden made of gold. They also found shields, leather goods, sandals, breastplates, and knives and other tools. The soldiers ignored the pleas of the Incas, and entered their sacred temples, stealing everything they could get their hands on. They counted the equivalent of 588,266 pesos in gold and 228,310 marks of silver, but that was only a fraction of what was there.[**]

The booty from those two cities made Pizarro and de Soto two of the richest men in Spain. De Soto would spend the rest of his life trying to find a treasure to match it.

[*] David Ewing Duncan, *Hernando de Soto: A Savage Quest in the Americas* (Norman, OK: University of Oklahoma Press, 1996), 158.

[**] Ibid., 185.

(continued from page 61)

competing for the same positions, and both were hot tempered. And Hernando Pizarro, too, was constantly stirring up trouble. De Soto was thinking of new worlds to conquer. He wanted to try for Chile, south of Peru. But King Charles had given that concession to Almagro. De Soto was not invited to participate. He was bitterly disappointed. Finally, Francisco Pizarro dismissed him.

De Soto, richer than he ever imagined, decided to return to Spain to ask the king for fresh lands to conquer. He boarded his ship, the *San Geronimo,* in 1536, filling it with his gold and silver, and headed for Spain.

Test Your Knowledge

1 Why did Pizarro and de Soto have to plan
   their Peruvian expedition in secret?
   a. They were defying a direct order from
      the king.
   b. They were both wanted fugitives.
   c. They feared angering Pedrarias
      Dávila.
   d. None of the above.

2 How was de Soto ultimately able to leave
   Nicaragua?
   a. Dávila relented and removed the ban
      on travel.
   b. De Soto departed without Dávila's
      knowledge.
   c. Conveniently for de Soto, Dávila died.
   d. None of the above.

3 Which of the following factors helped the
   Spaniards to conquer the Incas?
   a. The jungle terrain was harsh.
   b. The Inca Empire was in the midst of
      a civil war.
   c. The Incas had only a small army.
   d. None of the above.

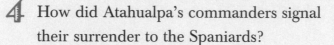

4 How did Atahualpa's commanders signal their surrender to the Spaniards?
   a. They made the sign of the cross.
   b. They broke their spears and arrows.
   c. They bowed to the Spaniards.
   d. None of the above.

5 Why was de Soto unable to stop the execution of Atahualpa?
   a. He lacked the authority.
   b. He was away investigating the rumor of a large Incan army preparing to attack.
   c. He was imprisoned when Atahualpa was killed.
   d. None of the above.

ANSWERS: 1. c; 2. c; 3. b; 4. a; 5. b

On to
La Florida

Twenty-two years after he left Spain, de Soto returned to Seville. He was 36 years old. He was famous now. A crowd of people stood on the dock to have a look at him.

De Soto wasted no time in finding a castle and numerous servants, including a grand master of ceremonies, pages, and footservants. He was very wealthy, but still was not satisfied. What he really wanted was honor and power. Pedrarias Dávila was dead, and Hernando de Soto decided to marry his daughter, Isabel de Bobadilla. Her dowry consisted of the cattle that her father had had in Panama and many slaves. But perhaps what de Soto wanted most from her was the political and social influence of her family. He was allowed now to be a member of the very elite Order of Santiago. De Soto asked to be a governor of Quito in Peru, but the Pizarros had already been given that office. Then he was turned down for the governorship of Guatemala.

A GOVERNOR NOW

In 1537 Charles I gave him the concession to conquer La Florida. He now had the title of *adelantado*, which means Spanish governor. He was also allowed to be the governor of Cuba.

Three other missions had gone to La Florida, and failed. Juan Ponce de León set sail in 1513. He was another man known to be cruel. He landed on the eastern coast, south of present-day Jacksonville, and called it La Florida. When he tried to make slaves of the Indians, they attacked, and Ponce de León left. He is associated with the fabled Fountain of Youth, but he never discovered it or was actually that interested in finding it. A court historian named Peter Martyr may have started the false rumor about the fountain.[21] Ponce de León returned to Florida in 1521, and was killed.

Another mission was led by Pánfilo de Narváez. He and his men disappeared in 1528. One of the four survivors of this ill-fated expedition returned to Spain to ask for the concession to Florida, but Hernando de Soto had already been granted it.

De Soto began to prepare for one of the largest and most expensive missions to leave Spain. He bought as many as five ships, if not more, which were loaded with everything from wine to gunpowder. De Soto's most faithful men went around the country getting people to join up.

De Soto made a trip back to Estremadura to spend time with his sisters. He managed to talk a relative of his mother's into going with him, along with a nephew. His niece's new husband also signed on. The fleet headed to Cuba on April 28, 1538. Once it arrived, de Soto and company spent several months organizing the expedition. Again, the governor lived like a king. He had a ranch, and a beautiful house in Havana that came with 18 household slaves. Around this time, de Soto and his partner from early on, Hernán Ponce de León, began to fight over the possessions that they had promised to divide equally. They parted enemies.

It was time for de Soto to focus on La Florida and how to approach it. He sent 50 men, led by Juan de Añasco, ahead to find a suitable place to land. They headed for the Gulf of Mexico side of Florida, where there were two natural harbors. They captured four Indians, who were forced to serve as guides and interpreters. It took them two months to sail back to Havana to report to de Soto.

The total number of people going on the mission numbered around 1,000.[22] Among them were 600 officers, soldiers, tradesmen, servants, and non-Indian slaves, pages, and prostitutes. There were 130 sailors and 240 horses. The ships set sail on May 18, 1539.[23]

THE MISSION SAILS

The ships sailed into a wide natural harbor on May 25. De Soto called it *Bahia de Espiritu Santo,* or the Bay of the Holy Spirit, to honor their arrival on a holy day, Whitsuntide.[24] Most historians agree that the harbor they entered was Tampa Bay. De Soto and his men, however, had no idea where they had landed. Birds were everywhere, and they admired the lush shoreline. But what was more interesting to them was the smoke that told them that Indians were nearby. The Indians had run away when they saw the fleet of ships approaching.

The next day, however, eight Indians showed up out of curiosity. The Spaniards and the Indians began fighting, and within moments two Indians and two horses were dead. De Soto led his men inland to the Indian village of Ocita, which had been abandoned. There, they set up camp. De Soto didn't waste any time. He walked to the beach and raised the flag of his king. He was claiming North America for the Spanish Crown. In fact, he was claiming 7.3 million square miles of land for Spain.[25] He was certain that he would leave this land loaded down with gold and other riches.

The expedition of Hernando de Soto makes its landing at Bahia de Espiritu Santo, or the Bay of the Holy Spirit. Most historians believe that the harbor de Soto entered was modern-day Tampa Bay.

But he had not taken into account the one million Indians who lived in the Southeast region of North America. As for the Indians, some along the coast had had the misfortune of seeing the Spaniards who had come before. But most went about their lives, not in the least aware of diseases and strangely clothed soldiers, guns and horses.

The Timucuans were the first tribe that the Spaniards came across. They were good at hiding from de Soto and his men, which frustrated them.

When the Spaniards did catch up to the Indians, de Soto learned what fierce fighters they were. They had a secret weapon—the longbow. Their bows were thick and six to seven feet long, and the men who shot the arrows were almost always accurate.[26]

When scouting parties went out, they could expect to run into a fight. During one of these scouting trips, the Spaniards found Juan Ortiz, a survivor of the Narváez expedition who had been captured by the Indians. Ortiz would remain with de Soto for a long time.

The Spaniards spent weeks creating a settlement. De Soto had not had any encouraging news about the gold he expected to find. But a little progress was being made with at least some of the Indians. One Indian leader, Mocoso, who was the patron to Juan Ortiz, invited de Soto to meet him. He explained that two other *caciques* (leaders)—Ocita and Urriparacoxi—were his enemies. He wanted to join with the Spaniards. De Soto admired Mocoso, the same way he had admired Atahualpa.

MARCHING NORTH

De Soto, after much thought, decided that he and his

men could not create a colony in Bahia de Espiritu Santo (Tampa). The area was too swampy. It was time to move on. They traveled in the usual conquista

Juan Ortiz

When de Soto and his men were in the Tampa Bay area, they had a hard time capturing the Timucuans. Even when they caught them, most were able to escape. One day, a group of de Soto's men were on horseback and came upon four Indians. One by one they knocked them down with their lances. When they came to the fourth, he cried out in Spanish, "Sirs, for the love of God and of St. Mary, do not kill me: I am a Christian, like you, and I am a native of Seville, and my name is Juan Ortiz." * When the horsemen came after him again, he kept screaming, "Seville!" The horsemen pulled the man up and raced back to camp.

Ortiz had been on the Narváez expedition 11 years earlier, but had returned to Cuba when the army went into the interior of La Florida. Back in Cuba, however, Narváez's wife asked Ortiz to go with a mission to find her missing husband. He agreed. When he and his fellow sailors arrived formation. The vanguard (the advance group made up of horsemen and sometimes foot soldiers) led, and another group of horsemen and foot soldiers,

along the coast, Ortiz and another man went ashore when they saw what looked like a letter hung on a tree. The Indians, who remembered Narváez, attacked them. Narváez had cut off the chief Ocita's nose and murdered his mother.

The Indians almost killed Ortiz. However, the cacique's daughter asked her father to spare his life. The chief agreed, but Ortiz was treated like a slave. Even worse, the chief Ocita began to beat him often. When the young princess learned that her father planned to sacrifice Ortiz to their gods, she warned him. She also helped him to sneak away late at night. Ortiz was taken in by another cacique, Mocoso, who was not friendly with Ocita. De Soto was amazed by Ortiz's story and had him join him and his men. He was an expert translator for de Soto.

* David Ewing Duncan, *Hernando de Soto: A Savage Quest in the Americas* (Norman, OK: University of Oklahoma Press, 1996), 259.

The chief's daughter tries to save Juan Ortiz, a survivor of the Narváez expedition who was captured by the Indians. One of de Soto's scouting parties later found Ortiz, who joined with de Soto and served as an interpreter with the Indians.

servants, and ladies followed. The rear guard rode in back. They traveled north from present-day Tampa Bay. They came upon the Great Ocale Swamp, entering the land of the Ocale Indians in July 1539.

De Soto and around 50 of his soldiers set out to explore. The Ocale Indians hid, just as the Ocita and Timucuan had. But that didn't stop them from attacking the Spaniards whenever they had the chance. De Soto and his men did find a three-month supply of corn and other food. And they met much more resistance from the Indians up ahead as they made their way to Apalachee, a seven-day hike.

De Soto was learning that La Florida was not Peru. In Peru, the natives had been willing to guide Pizarro and his men. De Soto must have expected the same reaction in North America, and for that reason did not bother to bring with him anyone who understood instrument navigation. He did not have good maps. This led to a lot of dependence on guesswork and on the Indians, who gave false information.

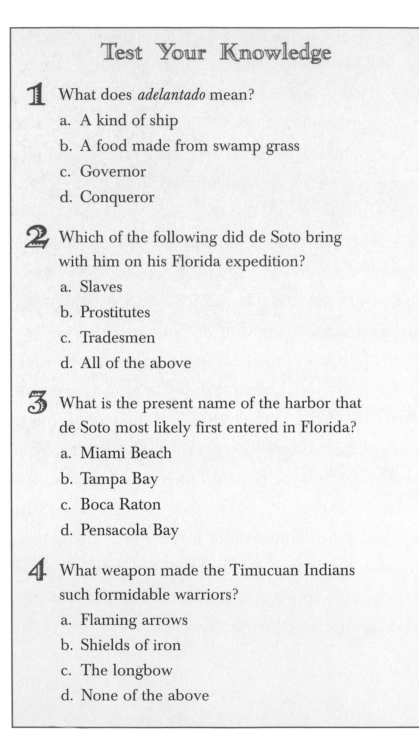

Test Your Knowledge

1 What does *adelantado* mean?

   a. A kind of ship

   b. A food made from swamp grass

   c. Governor

   d. Conqueror

2 Which of the following did de Soto bring with him on his Florida expedition?

   a. Slaves

   b. Prostitutes

   c. Tradesmen

   d. All of the above

3 What is the present name of the harbor that de Soto most likely first entered in Florida?

   a. Miami Beach

   b. Tampa Bay

   c. Boca Raton

   d. Pensacola Bay

4 What weapon made the Timucuan Indians such formidable warriors?

   a. Flaming arrows

   b. Shields of iron

   c. The longbow

   d. None of the above

5 Which of the following made it difficult
for de Soto and his expedition to travel
through Florida?
   a. Inaccurate maps
   b. False information from local Indians
   c. Frequent Indian attacks
   d. All of the above

ANSWERS: 1. c; 2. d; 3. b; 4. c; 5. d

Mississippian Culture

During this time, de Soto focused on his crusade to find gold or riches in North America at all costs. He and his men had crossed into a no-man's-land; they had been in the middle of two societies at war with each other. In what is now Tallahassee, they came to the chiefdom of Apalachee. This chiefdom belonged to a southeastern American culture that historians would later name the Mississippian Culture.

There are two ways of looking at the people and places the Spaniards encountered over four years. Tracing their journey, the names of the chiefdoms ring out: Ocute, Cofitachequi, Ilapi, Coosa (to name but a few). And there are the rivers—Congaree, Wateree, Catawba, Swannanoa—that the explorers used to get their bearings. But we get more of a sense of de Soto's travels when we follow his course from the names of the places that are familiar to us today. De Soto and his men went from Tampa Bay to Lakeland, Florida, to Gainesville and Tallahassee, and then onto Macon, Georgia; Camden, South Carolina; Marion, North Carolina; and so on.[27] They also crossed sections of the Blue Ridge Mountains, the Tennessee Valley, and the Appalachian Mountains. De Soto and his men, in fact, entered ten future U.S. states. It must be remembered that they had poor maps. From one Indian village to the next, de Soto would inquire about what lay ahead. It is amazing when looking at a U.S. map today to realize how much territory they covered.

But to fully understand the discovery of the Southeast, it might be time to reexamine the man who led the expedition. When Hernando de Soto arrived on the shores of North America, he already had a reputation for being a fierce conquistador. He was also known for his cunning nature and for his ill treatment of anyone who crossed him.

Author David Ewing Duncan described de Soto as "one of the toughest, most ruthless, most able conquistadors in the Indies. A man of thunder and passion, of towering ambition and brutal resolve,"[28] he represented everything good and evil about the conquistadors. Though he was entering one of the most unique and beautiful lands in the world at that time, de Soto could only think about precious metals.

The degree of destruction that de Soto and his men caused must be weighed against their discoveries, as they went from chiefdom to chiefdom. They looted villages and towns. De Soto thought nothing of kidnapping Indians and forcing them to be guides or slaves. This had been his practice for years. He would end up murdering tens of thousands of natives in the New World either through warfare,

Hernando de Soto leads his soldiers through the forest of Florida in 1539. Near Tallahassee, they reached Apalachee, a chiefdom that was home to at least 25,000 Indians and perhaps as many as 100,000.

starvation, or the diseases that he and his men transmitted to the natives.[29]

APALACHEE

De Soto and his men were quite disappointed that they had not found gold. They were constantly trying to capture Indians to guide them along the trails the Indians used. De Soto set his sights on the Apalachee, a kingdom so well run that it fed at least 25,000 and maybe as many as 100,000 people. The Apalachee worshiped the sun, and they loved bartering.[30]

They had been warned about the Spaniards moving closer, and the cacique sent hundreds of his Indians to fight the Spaniards. They had already fought the Spanish cavalry 11 years before when Narváez came through, so they were prepared for the horses. If all else failed, they had decided to run and burn everything behind them.

As de Soto and his men entered the thick forest, the Indians attacked. They fought for hours until they were in an open plain. De Soto, with his horses and tough soldiers, killed all of the attacking Indians. Though he had won for the moment, the Apalachee continued to attack the village where de Soto was staying.

Some Indians told de Soto about the cities in the north. They talked about powerful caciques, or chiefs, and the great mountains that today are called the Appalachian Mountains. The Spaniards were convinced that there was a link between mountains and gold because of their experience with the Incas. A boy whom they had kidnapped during a battle told them of great riches 13 days north. He was thinking about Cofitachequi, which was in South Carolina. This raised their hopes again. The boy, nicknamed Perico, would become a mascot for the Spanish soldiers on future travels. Where they counted on Ortiz to speak Spanish and the language of Timucuan, the boy could speak Timucuan and Muskogean.[31] This was important, for the Indians in North America did not share the same language. But the boy soon became confused about directions. De Soto captured Indians from the village of Patofa to guide him to Cofitachequi, but they, too, were soon lost. Finally, a scout arrived, saying he had found a village. He brought four captured natives. When they refused to act as guides, de Soto burned them.

At this time, in 1540, de Soto decided to send a small fleet of ships back to Cuba. He told the fleet's captain that if there was no word of him, the captain should return and keep cruising the coast until he showed up. De Soto headed north with the men who were left, convinced that he would find the golden empire.

THE INDIAN CULTURE

A vast Indian culture had existed along the valleys of the Mississippi, Cumberland, and Tennessee rivers and their tributaries. It was very active from around the eighth century to the fifteenth or sixteenth century.[32] In its heyday, cities arose from the Atlantic to Illinois and as far west as Oklahoma. Names of the sites that have been discovered in this century or the last include Etowah, Cahokia, and Moundville. Some of these centers had already started to decline when de Soto arrived, and by the time the next wave of explorers arrived, the culture had changed. It evolved into tribes like the Creek and the Cherokee a century after de Soto left.

De Soto and his men passed through many of these villages seeking gold. The people were not governed by anyone with absolute power. Instead, hundreds of small societies participated. Some of them were gatherers, and others depended on crops of maize (or corn), beans, or squash for their existence. Most of them were traders, and they exchanged pottery, conch shells, copper, and woven garments.

This Mississippian bowl is in the shape of a crested wood duck. The Mississippian Culture flourished from the eighth century to the fifteenth century.

People were able to live closer together because of the cultivation of maize and beans. Other foods that the Indians ate were fish, deer, turkey, berries, and other fruits.[33] They were organized into chiefdoms. Etowah and Coosa were two important ones that De Soto encountered. The community was usually divided into nine districts, and each one had a local chief. The chiefs reported to the Great Son.

Some of the centers, like Cahokia in Illinois and Moundville in Alabama, were larger and more complex social centers.

Most of them had large, flat-topped earthen mounds. They were placed near the villages, and

The Mississippi Valley

Nicknamed the Muddy Mississippi, the Mississippi River has shaped the valley that it runs through. It is one of the largest rivers in the Americas. Sometimes, this unpredictable river floods an area in the spring or summer, causing a lot of damage, but it blesses other areas by creating a richer soil with the sediment the river carries. The flooding created a rich soil, which worked well for the Indians who were starting to become farmers.

Two regions within the Mississippi Valley—the Yazoo Basin and the Central Valley—were heavily populated during the Middle Mississippian period (1000 to 1350). But by the time de Soto and his men passed by, the cultures had started to collapse. The Central Valley runs 500 miles on the western side of the river from the mouth supported temples and homes for the rulers, priests, and more elite members of their society. The mounds may have been used for defense, and important people were buried in some of them. Whatever their use, they were important to the

of the Ohio River to the Arkansas River. On the eastern side, the Yazoo Basin runs from an area just south of Memphis, Tennessee, down to Vicksburg, Mississippi.

The kingdom of Coosa was in the southern part of the Tennessee Valley. The Mississippian Indians thought it was a good place to live. Many clear rivers ran down from the mountains. Rainfall was abundant, and the Indians had a long growing season. There were many towns, and fields of corn and beans grew along the streams. There were wonderful fruit trees. Grapevines could be seen along the streams. In many ways, this area reminded the conquistadors of Spain. But de Soto was unable to understand that the land they crossed offered more abundance than any pots of gold.

Many of the Indian communities featured large, flat-topped mounds, like the one here at Cahokia in Illinois. The mounds supported temples and homes for the elite members of the society. Cahokia was one of the largest social centers of the Mississippian Culture.

townspeople. Some were built by hand over many years. The dirt had to be carried in baskets and put down bit by bit. The largest one at Cahokia rose to a height of 100 feet and covered 16 acres.

Test Your Knowledge

1 How many present-day states did de Soto's expedition enter?

  a. Three

  b. Six

  c. Ten

  d. None of the above

2 How did de Soto's men treat the Indian tribes they encountered?

  a. They treated the Indians as equals.

  b. They tortured, killed, enslaved, and robbed the Indians.

  c. They treated the Indians as trading partners.

  d. None of the above.

3 What are *caciques*?

  a. Indian chiefs

  b. Arrows

  c. Copper masks

  d. None of the above

4 Which of the following foods were staples of the Indians' diet?

  a. Maize and beans

  b. Deer and turkeys

  c. Fruits and berries

  d. All of the above

5 What was the use of the earthen mounds built by the Indians?

a. They supported homes for the elite and may have been used for defense.

b. They were built for spiritual rituals.

c. They were built to better save crops from floods.

d. None of the above.

ANSWERS: 1. c; 2. b; 3. a; 4. d; 5. a

The Changing Tide

De Soto and his men finally arrived in Cofitachequi, which was on a river in South Carolina. It was May 1, 1540. The food supply was dwindling, and de Soto was constantly concerned about having enough food for his men. The lack of food was another reason why he kept pushing from one village to the next. The *cacica*, or queen, at Cofitachequi welcomed him. She wore beautiful pearls and offered de Soto five or six long strands. This gave the Spaniards great hope.[34] They later found 200 pounds of pearls in graves, which they took.

They roamed around Cofitachequi but were mystified by the absence of people. It turned out that a plague had killed most of the people. The young queen apologized for the lack of food, though she was able to help out some. De Soto went all over looking for gold and realized that there was none in the area. His men suggested that they create a colony. De Soto would have none of it. It was just as well, because by the time the Spaniards left, the cacica refused to send her people to help carry supplies.

MILES AND MILES

De Soto marched with his men north to the present-day area of Hickory, North Carolina, and then to the Blue Ridge Mountains at Marion. From there they dropped into the valley of Asheville, North Carolina, which had been cleared by the Indians. It was spectacular country. Crossing the mountains was extremely difficult. De Soto turned toward Coca.[35] The word had spread through the communities that de Soto was a cruel man.

At this point, the expedition consisted of 550 men, traveling an average of 16 miles a day. They marched on to Chiaha, 25 miles east of present-day Knoxville, Tennessee. To their great relief, there was plenty of corn. The Indians there had heard all about the strangers so focused on finding yellow and white metals. The advice they received from the other tribes was to give the Spaniards what they wanted and not to engage in battle. This worked until de Soto asked them to hand over their women. When the Indians moved their women and children to safer ground, de Soto was angry, but for the first time he decided not to destroy them. He asked for men to carry the Spanish possessions instead.

De Soto seemed to relax for a time. He still had three years to carry out his contract with the king of Spain. He figured that he would catch up with the returning ships in the near future. He had led his men over 1,300 miles of unknown territory. That in itself was an amazing feat.

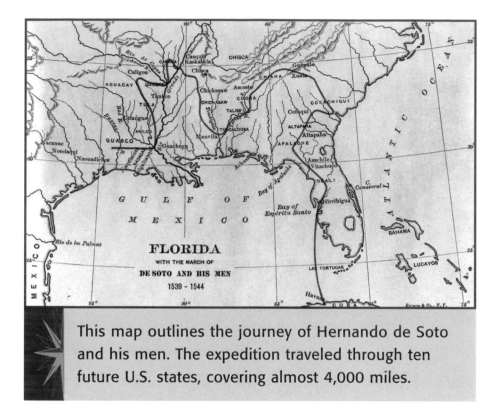

This map outlines the journey of Hernando de Soto and his men. The expedition traveled through ten future U.S. states, covering almost 4,000 miles.

De Soto came to the capital of the largest empire in the south, the land of the Coosa, located in northwestern Georgia. Coosa stretched for 200 miles, extending into present-day Tennessee and Alabama.[36] Anywhere from 11 to 17 villages were built along riverbanks. Several mounds occupied the center of the village of Coosa. As usual, when de Soto was leaving a place, he would take the chief with him for protection. De Soto wanted to march south to meet his supply ship. He took the young chief and his sister. They were kept in chains. Finally, he let the young chief go but kept the girl. The Indians had had it. The ruling family of Coosa decided to fight the strangers. The Coosa sent messages far and wide through the network of Indians about the great threat of the outsiders. De Soto and his men did not know that their former prisoner was doing this.

THE BATTLE OF MABILA

The Atahachi lived in the area of present-day Montgomery, Alabama. The Atahachi chief was named Tascalusa. He was a giant of a man. He stood six and a half feet tall. He had highly developed warriors under him. He was also more aware than the other Indian leaders of how de Soto liked to enter a town with only a few men to prove his boldness.

De Soto entered the town, put the very popular Tascalusa in chains, and forced him to march. The chief was no fool. He watched the stranger. Soon, he realized that de Soto and his leaders had become a little careless. The chief spoke to de Soto and his men about the beautiful women who were waiting for them at the fortress of Mabila.

De Soto had been in North America for 17 months. He and his men decided to take up Tascalusa's offer to go to Mabila. When they arrived, de Soto was handed gifts. There was singing and dancing, and then young women came out and began dancing. Tascalusa told de Soto that he wanted to remain in Mabila, but de Soto said no. Then Tascalusa asked permission to enter a house. He refused to come out, even when de Soto tried to talk to him.

De Soto sent one of his men to enter the house, and when he did de Soto saw that the house was full of warriors. De Soto and his men started to retreat, leaving behind their baggage. De Soto was caught off guard. He fell twice as he made his way to his horsemen. Five Spaniards were killed immediately, and all the others inside were wounded. Their armor prevented more deaths. Many of the Indian porters with the de Soto expedition began stealing the Spaniards' swords, baggage and supplies and joining the Indians.

Later, de Soto figured that thousands of Indians had been waiting inside the fortress. De Soto decided to fight back. He and his men rushed up to the palisades, then pretended to run away. The Indians ran out to shoot arrows at them, but the men on horse-back turned quickly and killed most of the Indians. The Indians inside the fortress had prepared for battle, but they weren't ready for de Soto's tactics.

FIRE

De Soto and his men rushed the palisades. From then on the battle was fast and furious. De Soto and his men attacked over and over. The Indians put up a strong resistance. Then de Soto's men managed to climb over the palisades and set fire to the houses. Many Indians were burned alive. De Soto felt an arrow go deeply into his left hip. He didn't stop. The battle raged for seven hours. The Indians were losing, and the women began fighting, along with their children. No one wanted to surrender.

When it ended after nine hours, everything was burned. All the Spanish equipment was gone. Most of the Indians were dead. Some have estimated that 2,500 died there. The Inca soldier-poet, Garcilaso de la Vega, who wrote about de Soto's expedition in the late 1500s, put the number at 11,000 Indians.[37] No one ever saw Tascalusa again. Everyone believed that he died in the fire. His son's body was found.

(continued on page 102)

Animals

Among the fleet of ships that sailed to La Florida was a special one carrying horses, dogs, and pigs. Goats, sheep, and cattle would be brought over later.

The horses that de Soto brought to the New World were bred on the Barbary Coast of North Africa and brought to Spain by the Muslims. They resembled modern Arabian horses. They had wide foreheads, arched necks with long manes, and flowing tails. They were small and could carry heavy loads for long distances at rapid speeds. De Soto at first rode a dappled gray whose name was Aceytuno, named after the man who gave him the horse. The Spanish conquistadors used saddles designed by the Moors. The horses gave the conquistadors the advantage of speed when fighting the Indians. And they could assault their enemies from their saddles.

The Spaniards also brought with them large dogs of the mastiff family. They were used to herd animals, to hunt, and to terrorize men. They were muscular and had short hair. They could travel long distances without tiring. Another breed of dog that de Soto brought was the greyhound. They were war dogs, and were used to hunt and attack deer and other wild animals. The third kind of dog the Spaniards brought was a big attack dog called the alano, which was a mixture of breeds that included the mastiff and Irish wolfhound.

The dogs were vicious. They were trained to hunt down captives who were set free to try to escape, as though they were wild beasts. When the dogs caught the Indians, they ate them. They generally attacked a man's stomach and disemboweled him. Or they went after a man's genitals.[*]

The pigs the Spaniards liked to eat were like wild boars. They were good at defending themselves with their big tusks. The pigs ended up doing better on de Soto's long expedition than the dogs and horses. They could eat anything—plants, mushrooms, even snakes. They were easy to lead. Their sense of hearing was so acute that they could warn the soldiers when someone was coming. They were good swimmers, and they could move quickly when pushed. A female pig could give birth to a litter of 12, and sometimes she had two litters in a year.[**]

[*] Charles Hudson, *Knights of Spain, Warriors of the Sun* (Athens, GA: The University of Georgia Press, 1997), 75.

[**] Ibid., 77.

(continued from page 99)

The Indians had not understood the advantage the soldiers had with their armor and their horses. It was horrible enough that every fighting man in the region was either hurt or dead, but what no one realized at the time was that the Atahachi culture—their knowledge about crops and architecture and government—was also gone, never to be regained.

Twenty-two Spanish soldiers were dead, with about 250 wounded. The battle was one of the bloodiest fought in 500 years between Europeans and Indians. De Soto was horrified that he had lost all of his equipment and baggage. He was also left with half his army wounded. They needed time to regroup. He had had word that Spanish ships were waiting for him at Ochuse 136 miles away. He tried to keep the information from his men, but they learned of it anyway. Many of them wanted to leave. De Soto thought of this as mutiny. He could not stand to go back to Cuba and Spain with nothing to show for his efforts. Even his pearls were gone.

De Soto decided to continue the expedition. He was obsessed with finishing his mission of finding gold. He refused to ask the men what they wanted. Somehow he got his army to go with him. Some

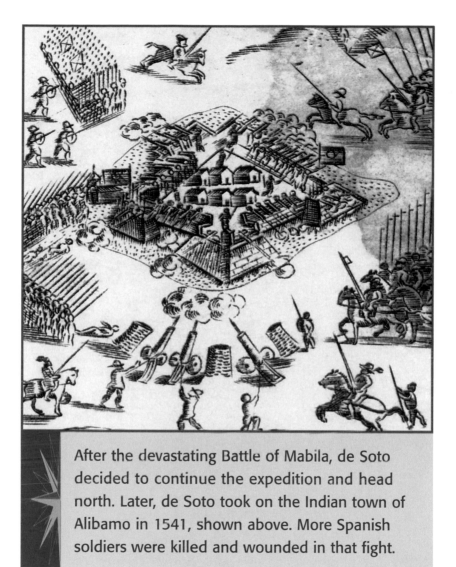

After the devastating Battle of Mabila, de Soto decided to continue the expedition and head north. Later, de Soto took on the Indian town of Alibamo in 1541, shown above. More Spanish soldiers were killed and wounded in that fight.

think he told them that the only way of surviving was to go north with him. They took off into the wilderness, crossing the Alabama River near present-day Selma.

Test Your Knowledge

1 What killed most of the Indians at
Cofitachequi?

a. De Soto and his men

b. A plague

c. A flood

d. A fire

2 How did de Soto react in Chiaha when
the Indians refused to give him their
women?

a. He massacred the Indians.

b. He took the chief hostage.

c. He instead asked for men to work
as porters.

d. None of the above.

3 How did Tascalusa try to trick de Soto?

a. He told de Soto that he knew of a
treasure in gold.

b. He used the promise of women to lure
de Soto into an ambush.

c. He led de Soto's men in circles until
they were lost in the woods.

d. None of the above.

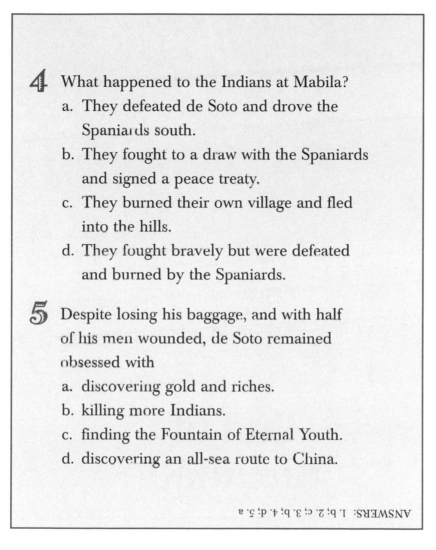

4 What happened to the Indians at Mabila?
   a. They defeated de Soto and drove the
      Spaniards south.
   b. They fought to a draw with the Spaniards
      and signed a peace treaty.
   c. They burned their own village and fled
      into the hills.
   d. They fought bravely but were defeated
      and burned by the Spaniards.

5 Despite losing his baggage, and with half
   of his men wounded, de Soto remained
   obsessed with
   a. discovering gold and riches.
   b. killing more Indians.
   c. finding the Fountain of Eternal Youth.
   d. discovering an all-sea route to China.

ANSWERS: 1. b; 2. c; 3. b; 4. d; 5. a

End of the Road

After he left Mabila, de Soto had a choice. He went north, but he could have led his men south. In what is now Pensacola Bay, Florida, Spanish ships were waiting. At that point, he could have either resupplied or returned to Cuba.

He and his men went northwest where they came upon the chiefdom of Apafalaya. There, the chief himself was forced to lead them farther. He led them through swamps and rivers to northern Mississippi. They spent the winter in Chicaca (later the land of the Chickasaw). It snowed, and many of the soldiers had to sleep outside. There was a supply of food, however, and they built small houses. The natives and the Spaniards got along for a while. But then the natives were offered some pork, as de Soto still had pigs. The Indians started stealing the hogs. Three Indians were caught, and de Soto killed two of them while cutting off the hands of the third [38]

On the day de Soto planned to leave, the Indians attacked. They set fire to all of the houses and the sheds that protected the animals. Twelve Spaniards, 57 horses, and 400 pigs died. Only one Indian died. When the Spaniards counted their losses, they realized that all of their saddles and shields had burned in the fire. Most of their clothes were gone. They learned from a few captured prisoners that the members of their tribe had sworn to their gods to die in their attempt to kill the Spaniards.

De Soto decided to move to the chiefdom of the Chicazilla. He and his men made clothing out of dressed deerskins. Slowly, using local materials, they made new saddles and shields, and built lances from the ash trees. De Soto, full of revenge, went after the Indians, and later claimed to have killed all of them. But that was not the case. The Chicazilla came back to attack, but de Soto and his men were able to get away.

The situation only got worse. De Soto next picked a fight with the Alibamos, who had prepared a trap for the Spanish conquistadors. Thirty of de Soto's men were wounded, and 15 died days later. This time de Soto's men thought their fearless leader had shown poor military judgment.

It was 1541. The Spaniards traveled for eight and a half days when they saw no one. Finally, they came to the chiefdom of Quizquiz. It was near the Mississippi River, south of present-day Memphis. They arrived exhausted and worried. The first thing de Soto did was capture 300 women while the men were away. The cacique, instead of fighting, explained that they were surrendering. He told de Soto of a town up ahead

A postcard shows de Soto discovering the Mississippi River. What he and his men discovered was the inland part of the Mississippi. They next spent a month cutting down trees and building four big boats to cross the wide river.

that had plenty of maize, and de Soto and his men left.

The Spaniards saw the Mississippi River for the first time around May 15, 1541. What they were discovering was the inland part of the river.[39] The mouth had been sighted and explored years earlier. They couldn't believe how wide the river was. It was about a mile and a half wide, and over 100 feet deep.

They spent almost a month cutting trees down and building four big, flat-bottomed boats. Taking their horses, they climbed on, rowing as hard as they could. They landed across the river on the banks of present-day Arkansas.

This time de Soto hoped to make friends with the Indians they met. They entered the village of Casqui toward the end of June. De Soto and his men built a cross and prayed. Rain came, saving the corn crop. The Casqui were impressed. They asked de Soto to help them fight a neighboring tribe, the Pacaha. De Soto had heard that the Pacaha had gold. By the time de Soto reached that chiefdom, the Indians had fled. The soldiers found cloaks, bearskins, and blankets. The gold that they were hoping to find turned out to be copper.

They continued to the largest town yet, Quiguate, where they stayed for 21 days. De Soto sent his scouts out in all directions. He did not know where to go next. Reports came in that a vast prairie lay to the north. He had already visited the kingdoms in the east. The south led back to the sea, and he didn't want to head there. The only option was west. The Indians talked about the other sea that lay beyond the wilderness he would have to cross. He thought it was the Pacific Ocean, but he was not even close. From the very beginning, the maps de Soto carried with him only had vague information about Florida.

The journey was a miserable one. The soldiers caught fish for food, but the area was swampy. They saw buffalo for the first time and killed them for meat. Then they were in the Ozarks. They continued to steal food and Indians in each town they entered. De Soto's men were exhausted and growing more desperate.

In October, de Soto and some of his men went to investigate Tula. The Indians attacked them immediately. The natives were used to killing buffalo with poles that were like lances, and they could use these to kill the horses. De Soto realized that these people were not like the more gentle Mississippian farmers. They were much tougher. On top of that, the Spaniards entered a sea of grass. De Soto looked around and realized that it was unlikely he would find any wealthy kingdoms. He also realized that the Pacific Ocean was far away.

Winter was approaching, and de Soto hoped to find a town he could take over. It was to be their third winter in La Florida. De Soto also thought about returning to Mississippi. So far, he had lost 250 men and 150 horses. What he ended up doing was spending a fiercely cold winter in Arkansas. The person he had perhaps counted on the most, Juan Ortiz, died. The winter of 1542 was long. De Soto had time to think. He had invested almost everything he had in this quest for gold. He had not found any precious metals, and he had not established a town, a trade route, or a mission.

In March, de Soto and his 400 men and 40 horses went down the Arkansas River to where it met the Mississippi. They found plenty of maize, beans, and dried plums. There were chiefdoms in the area, but he learned that there were none to the south. The cacique of the Mississippian empire called Quigaltam demanded to know what he was doing there. De Soto realized that he and his men could not fight the Indians even if they had wanted to. He also learned that they could not get to the Gulf of Mexico. He had thought if they could go there, they could find their way to Cuba.

At this point the unimaginable happened. Hernando de Soto became ill with a fever. His spirit and energies were drained. From his sickbed, though, he sent word to the cacique of Quigaltam that he was a god and that he should come to visit him. Even in illness, de Soto did not change. The cacique sent back scornful words, saying that "it was not his custom to visit anyone, but rather to be visited and served."[40] De Soto was furious. How dare an Indian try to display power over a conquistador.

De Soto was not done yet. He sent his men to a village, ordering them to attack with all their might. His men obeyed, killing 100 women, men, and children who had no defenses.

De Soto knew he was dying. He chose a loyal follower, Luis de Moscoso Alvarado, who had been with him in Peru, to take control. On May 21, 1542, Hernando de Soto died. He was 42 years old.

At first his men buried him, but then they worried that the Indians would know their god-leader had died. They dug him up, put his body into a hollow log, filled the log with sand, and carried it out into the middle of the Mississippi River.[41]

An engraving depicts the Spaniards burying Hernando de Soto in the Mississippi River in 1542. They buried him there so that the Indians would not know that de Soto had died.

The survivors, led by Luis de Moscoso, faced a choice. They could go overland to Mexico or they could go down the Mississippi River to its mouth and sail to Cuba. What they could not know was that the captain of the ship de Soto had ordered to cruise the shores was doing just that. He never stopped searching for them until 1543 when he learned that they had been found. At first, Moscoso and the men had chosen to go overland. In June 1542, they set out for Mexico. The chiefdoms were poor, and there was little food. They made their way to Texas until they came in contact with the Caddo people. The weather was hot. There wasn't much water. And they were crossing prairies. They turned around and headed back to the Mississippi River.

This time they would build boats and sail down the river. They sailed for 750 miles, often being

What Came After

The conquistadors of Spain had more practical matters in mind than the American explorers, like Meriwether Lewis, who began crossing the country in the eighteenth and nineteenth centuries. Lewis and others were not seeking gold, but instead were obsessed with discovering new rivers that would lead them to the Pacific Ocean. When the Spanish first saw the majestic Mississippi River they thought of it as something to cross, not as a wonder of nature.

Artists and writers in the late nineteenth century depicted Hernando de Soto as a heroic figure. In those years, the Spanish conquests were viewed as the triumph of European civilization over people who were inferior in every way. Paintings of him hang in museums and courthouses across the United States. In Florida, he remains a hero. Though many were taught to believe that he discovered the Mississippi River, the truth is that Spanish explorers had found it around 1510.

What Hernando de Soto and his men did not grasp because of their obsession with gold was that the land they were crossing was the real find. Game was plentiful. The hardwood forests of Georgia and Florida were extraordinary, as were the meadows and lowlands and mountains they crossed. De Soto's men were right to suggest founding a colony. Perhaps they could see the potential of the magnificent landscape.

It wasn't until 1565 that a Spanish fleet came to the coast of northern Florida and finally established a colony called St. Augustine. What the newcomers to America found in the areas de Soto and his men had "conquered" were lost villages. Then the missionaries started arriving in 1568, which exposed the Indians to additional diseases like mumps. Instead of helping the natives, they killed most of them.

attacked by the Indians. They entered the Gulf of Mexico and followed the coast. They reached Veracruz, Mexico, on September 10, 1543. They had been given up for dead. About half of them had survived. It had taken them four years and four months to cover almost 4,000 miles in North America.

"In the English speaking world Soto has had a reputation of a shining knight. . . . The Anglo-Saxons engaged in this image-building of Soto mainly for the puerile reason that Soto could be considered an explorer of the United States. . . . Still, Soto does stand out as a knight of sorts, hasty, dashing and gallant."[42] That statement by the historian James Lockhart sums up the conflicted opinions surrounding Hernando de Soto. People want to believe that he was a hero. In Florida, celebrations are held in his name. Schools, islands and parks are named after the man who was the first to cross most of the Southeast. But that honor is forever dimmed by what we know about him as a human being.

Test Your Knowledge

1 How did the Spaniards replace the saddles and shields burned at Chicaca?

  a. They used local materials for shields and saddles, and made lances of ash trees.

  b. They forced the Indians to make them new shields of copper and saddles of deer hide.

  c. They never replaced their shields and rode their horses bareback.

  d. None of the above.

2 How did the Spaniards face the challenge of the Mississippi River?

  a. They turned back rather than risk swimming across.

  b. They found a shallow ford and marched across.

  c. They built large, flat-bottomed boats and rowed across.

  d. None of the above.

3 How much gold did de Soto find during his journey in North America?

  a. Only a few trinkets

  b. Enough to satisfy the king of Spain

  c. A small fortune

  d. None at all

4 How did Hernando de Soto die?

  a. He was killed in an Indian attack.

  b. He drowned in the Mississippi River.

  c. He died of fever and disease.

  d. He was killed by his own men.

5 After de Soto's death, how did his men return to their countrymen?

  a. They marched south through what is now Florida.

  b. They sailed the Mississippi to the Gulf of Mexico, then to Veracruz, Mexico.

  c. They marched east, to the Atlantic, where Spanish ships were waiting.

  d. None of the above.

ANSWERS: 1. a; 2. c; 3. d; 4. c; 5. b

1492   Christopher Columbus sails to the Caribbean and claims the land of the Americas for Spain.

1500   Hernando de Soto is born.

1513   Juan Ponce de León discovers Florida.

1514   De Soto sails to Panama with Pedrarias Dávila.

1521   De Soto becomes a captain and a plantation owner in Nata, Panama.

1524   De Soto is a battalion leader under Francisco Hernández de Córdoba in the conquest of Nicaragua.

1500 Hernando de Soto is born.

1514 De Soto sails to Panama with Pedrarias Dávila.

1534 Francisco Pizarro names de Soto the lieutenant governor of Cuzco.

1500

1524 De Soto is a battalion leader under Francisco Hernández de Córdoba in the conquest of Nicaragua.

1531 The expedition to conquer Peru begins.

1527 Francisco Companon, de Soto's business partner, dies of fever.

1529 De Soto and Hernán Ponce de León sign a contract agreeing to aid in the conquest of Peru.

1531 Pedrarias Dávila dies at age 90.

1531 The expedition to conquer Peru begins.

1532 The Inca leader, Atahualpa, is captured and held hostage.

1533 Atahualpa is executed.

1534 Francisco Pizarro names de Soto the lieutenant governor of Cuzco.

1537 King Charles of Spain grants de Soto permission to conquer La Florida.

1542 De Soto comes down with a fever and dies on May 21 at Guachoya on the Mississippi River.

1540 De Soto marches through Georgia, South Carolina, North Carolina, Tennessee, and Alabama.

1542

1539 De Soto departs for Florida on May 18, and lands on May 25. He and his army leave the Tampa Bay area and march up the peninsula to the kingdom of Apalachee.

1541 De Soto reaches the Mississippi River and explores west.

1536 De Soto leaves for Spain.

1537 King Charles of Spain grants de Soto permission to conquer La Florida.

1538 De Soto leaves Spain and travels to Cuba.

1539 De Soto departs for Florida on May 18, and lands on May 25; De Soto and his army leave the Tampa Bay area and march up the peninsula to the kingdom of Apalachee.

1540 De Soto marches through Georgia, South Carolina, North Carolina, Tennessee, and Alabama.

1541 De Soto reaches the Mississippi River and explores west.

1542 De Soto comes down with a fever and dies on May 21 at Guachoya on the Mississippi River. Before his death, he names Luis de Moscoso Alvarado as leader; Moscoso tries to reach Mexico by marching the army through Texas.

1543 Moscoso and the army build boats and sail down the Mississippi to the Gulf of Mexico to escape from *La Florida*.

Chapter 1
Conquering an Empire

1. David Ewing Duncan, *Hernando de Soto: A Savage Quest in the Americas* (Norman, OK: University of Oklahoma Press, 1996), 132.

2. Patricia Galloway, ed., *The Hernando de Soto Expedition: History, Historiography, and "Discovery" in the Southeast* (Lincoln, NE, and London: University of Nebraska Press, 1997), Curt Lamar, "Hernando de Soto Before Florida: A Narrative," 186.

3. Duncan, *Hernando de Soto: A Savage Quest in the Americas,* 132–133.

4. Galloway, *The Hernando de Soto Expedition: History, Historiography, and "Discovery" in the Southeast,* Curt Lamar, "Hernando de Soto Before Florida: A Narrative," 187.

5. Duncan, *Hernando de Soto: A Savage Quest in the Americas,* 146.

6. Galloway, *The Hernando de Soto Expedition: History, Historiography, and "Discovery" in the Southeast,* Curt Lamar, "Hernando de Soto Before Florida: A Narrative," 192.

Chapter 2
The Boy Adventurer

7. Duncan, *Hernando de Soto: A Savage Quest in the Americas,* xx.

8. Ibid., 8.

9. Garcilaso de la Vega, *The Florida of the Inca,* translated and edited by John Grier Varner and Jeannette Johnson Varner (Austin, TX: University of Texas Press, 1951), xxi.

10. Duncan, *Hernando de Soto: A Savage Quest in the Americas,* 18.

Chapter 3
Conquering Nicaragua

11. Duncan, *Hernando de Soto: A Savage Quest in the Americas,* 52.

12. Ibid., 73.

13. Galloway, *The Hernando de Soto Expedition: History, Historiography, and "Discovery" in the Southeast,* Curt Lamar, "Hernando de Soto Before Florida: A Narrative," 192.

Chapter 4
The Central America Years

14. Paul E. Hoffman, "Hernando de Soto: A Brief Biography," in *The De Soto Chronicles,* 2 vols., Lawrence A. Clayton, ed., (Tuscaloosa, AL: The University of Alabama Press, 1993), vol. 1, p. 429.

15. Galloway, *The Hernando de Soto Expedition: History, Historiography, and "Discovery" in the Southeast,* Ralph H. Vigil, "The Expedition and the Struggle for Justice," 346.

16. Ibid., 336.

17. Duncan, *Hernando de Soto: A Savage Quest in the Americas,* 109.

Chapter 5
Discovery of Peru

18. Galloway, *The Hernando de Soto Expedition: History, Historiography, and "Discovery" in the Southeast,* Curt Lamar, "Hernando de Soto Before Florida: A Narrative," 184.
19. Duncan, *Hernando de Soto: A Savage Quest in the Americas,* 121.
20. Ibid., 153.

Chapter 6
On to *La Florida*

21. Duncan, *Hernando de Soto: A Savage Quest in the Americas,* 128.
22. Galloway, *The Hernando de Soto Expedition: History, Historiography, and "Discovery" in the Southeast,* Ignacio Avellaneda, "Hernando de Soto and His Florida Fantasy," 213.
23. Duncan, *Hernando de Soto: A Savage Quest in the Americas,* 243.
24. De la Vega, John Grier Varner and Jeannette Johnson Varner, eds., *The Florida of the Inca,* 59.
25. Duncan, *Hernando de Soto: A Savage Quest in the Americas,* 251.
26. Ibid., 254.

Chapter 7
Mississippian Culture

27. Jerald T. Milanich and Susan Milbrath, eds., *First Encounters: Spanish Explorations in the Caribbean and the United States, 1492–1570* (Gainesville, FL: University of Florida Press, 1989), 84–89.

28. Duncan, *Hernando de Soto: A Savage Quest in the Americas,* 330.
29. Duncan, *Hernando de Soto: A Savage Quest in the Americas,* xix.
30. Duncan, *Hernando de Soto: A Savage Quest in the Americas,* 297.
31. Galloway, *The Hernando de Soto Expedition: History, Historiography, and "Discovery" in the Southeast,* Jay K. Johnson, "From Chiefdom to Tribe in Mississippi," 300.
32. Charles Hudson, *The Southeastern Indians* (Knoxville, TN: The University of Tennessee Press, 1976), 36.
33. Ibid., 70.

Chapter 8
The Changing Tide

34. Ann Graham Gaines, *Hernando de Soto and the Spanish Search for Gold in World History* (Berkeley Heights, NJ: Enslow Publishers, Inc., 2002), 68.
35. Galloway, *The Hernando de Soto Expedition: History, Historiography, and "Discovery" in the Southeast,* Charles Hudson, "The Historical Significance of the Soto Route," 317.
36. Gaines, *Hernando de Soto and the Spanish Search for Gold in World History,* 72.
37. De la Vega, John Grier Varner and Jeannette Johnson Varner, eds., *The Florida of the Inca,* 379.

Chapter 9
End of the Road

38. Galloway, *The Hernando de Soto Expedition: History, Historiography, and "Discovery" in the Southeast*, Ralph H. Vigil, "The Expedition and the Struggle for Justice," 346.

39. Charles Hudson, *Knights of Spain, Warriors of the Sun* (Athens, GA: The University of Georgia Press, 1997), 349.

40. Galloway, *The Hernando de Soto Expedition: History, Historiography, and "Discovery" in the Southeast*, Ralph H. Vigil, "The Expedition and the Struggle for Justice," 348.

41. Duncan, *Hernando de Soto: A Savage Quest in the Americas*, 420.

42. Galloway, *The Hernando de Soto Expedition: History, Historiography, and "Discovery" in the Southeast*, Ignacio Avellaneda, "Hernando de Soto and His Florida Fantasy," 218.

De la Vega, Garcilaso. *The Florida of the Inca*, translated and edited by John Grier Varner and Jeannette Johnson Varner. Austin, TX: University of Texas Press, 1951.

Duncan, David Ewing. *Hernando de Soto: A Savage Quest in the Americas*. Norman, OK: University of Oklahoma Press, 1996.

Galloway, Patricia, ed. *The Hernando de Soto Expedition: History, Historiography, and "Discovery" in the Southeast.* Lincoln, NE, and London: University of Nebraska Press, 1997.

Gaines, Ann Graham. *Hernando de Soto and the Spanish Search for Gold in World History.* Berkeley Heights, NJ: Enslow Publishers, 2002.

Hoffman, Paul E., "Hernando de Soto: A Brief Biography," in *The De Soto Chronicles*, 2 vols., Lawrence A. Clayton, Vernon J. Knight, Edward C. Moore, eds. Tuscaloosa, AL: The University of Alabama Press, 1993.

Hudson, Charles. *Knights of Spain, Warriors of the Sun: Hernando de Soto and the South's Ancient Chiefdoms*. Athens, GA: The University of Georgia Press, 1997.

Hudson, Charles. *The Southeastern Indians*. Knoxville, TN: The University of Tennessee Press, 1976.

Milanich, Jerald T. and Susan Milbrath, eds. *First Encounters: Spanish Explorations in the Caribbean and the United States, 1492–1570.* Gainesville, FL: University of Florida Press, 1989.

Books

Gaines, Ann Graham. *Hernando de Soto and the Spanish Search for Gold in World History.* Berkeley Heights, NJ: Enslow Publishers, 2002.

Gallagher, Jim. *Hernando de Soto and the Exploration of Florida.* Philadelphia: Chelsea House Publishers, 2000.

Galloway, Patricia, ed. *The Hernando de Soto Expedition: History, Historiography, and "Discovery" in the Southeast.* Lincoln, NE, and London: University of Nebraska Press, 1997.

Pancella, Peggy. *Hernando de Soto.* Chicago, IL: Heinemann Library, 2003.

Websites

An Introduction to North America's Native People
www.cabrillo.edu/~crsmith/mississ.html

Incas and Conquistadors
www.hc09.dial.pipex.com/incas/home.shtml

De Soto National Memorial, National Park Service
www.nps.gov/deso/

The Story of the Conquistadors
www.bbc.co.uk/history/discovery/exploration/conquistadors_01.shtml

Janet Hubbard-Brown has written many books for children and young adults, including *The Labonte Brothers* and a biography of Geoffrey Chaucer for Chelsea House. She also writes adult mysteries and teaches writing in Vermont, where she has lived for 20 years.

William H. Goetzmann is the Jack S. Blanton, Sr. Chair in History and American Studies at the University of Texas, Austin. Dr. Goetzmann was awarded the Joseph Pulitzer and Francis Parkman Prizes for American History, 1967, for *Exploration and Empire: The Explorer and the Scientist in the Winning of the American West.* In 1999, he was elected a member of the American Philosophical Society, founded by Benjamin Franklin in 1743, to honor achievement in the sciences and humanities.